The

Programmer's Handbook

Thom Hogan

Brady Communications Company, Inc.
A Prentice-Hall Publishing Company
Bowie, MD 20715

Kai Fa Book Company
Taipei, Taiwan

The

Programmer's
Handbook

有著作權・不准翻印

台內著字第　　　號

原著者： Thom Hogan
發行人：甘　　　吉　　　雄
發行所：智　　邦　書　　局
　　　　台北市重慶南路一段86號
　　　　行政院新聞局局版台業字第1262號
總經銷：開　發　圖　書　有　限　公　司
　　　　台北市重慶南路一段86號
　　　　電話 3113551・3818935
　　　　郵撥帳戶： 0016894─0 號
印刷所：吉　豐　印　製　有　限　公　司
　　　　板橋市三民路二段正隆巷46弄7號

中華民國 74 年　　月一版
實價NT $
ISBN 0-89303-365-0

Dedication

This book is dedicated to those who had to put up with my antics while I wrote it: Maureen Harris, for pretending to not notice when I didn't write; my mother, Yvonne Hogan, who was sure that I was going to visit soon; my father, Tom Hogan, for wondering if I was ever going to come help him build the new family home in Hawaii; and to Terry Anderson, who kept hoping that I would really finish this book in the ridiculously short amount of time I promised I would.

Publishing Director: David Culverwell
Acquisitions Editor: Terrell Anderson
Production Editor/Text Design: Michael J. Rogers
Art Director/Cover Design: Don Sellers
Manufacturing Director: John Komsa

Typesetting: Harper Graphics, Waldorf, MD
Printing: R. R. Donnelley & Sons Company, Harrisonburg, VA
Copy Editor: Carol Thorsten-Stein

Limits of Liability and Disclaimer of Warranty

The author and publisher of this book have used their best efforts in preparing this book and programs contained in it. These efforts include the development, research, and testing of the programs to determine their effectiveness. The author and the publisher make no warranty of any kind, expressed or implied, with regard to these programs, the text, or the documentation contained in this book. The authors and the publisher shall not be liable in any event for claims of incidental or consequential damages in connection with, or arising out of, the furnishing, performance, or use of the text or the programs. The programs contained in this book are intended for the use of the original purchaser.

Note to Authors

Do you have a manuscript or software program related to personal computers? Do you have an idea for developing such a project? If so, we would like to hear from you. The Brady Company produces a complete range of books and applications software for the personal computer market. We invite you to write to David Culverwell, Publishing Director, Brady Communications Company, Inc., Bowie, MD 20715.

Trademarks of Material Mentioned in This Text

UNIX is a trademark of AT&T Bell Laboratories.

CP/M is a trademark of Digital Research.

MS-DOS is a trademark of Microsoft Corporation.

Other trade names used in this text may be trademarked by the provider.

About the Author

Having already explored promising careers as an architect, professional musician, and filmmaker, Thom Hogan discovered computers in 1977 and hasn't been the same since. A respected authority on small computers, Thom is mostly known for his numerous books and manuals (*CP/M User Guide, Discover FORTH, The c Programmer's Handbook, InfoWorld's Guide to the Apple II, The TRS-80 Model 100 User Guide, The Osborne 1 Technical Manual*) and for his editorial work at *InfoWorld* and *The Portable Companion*. Amidst all that prolific writing, Thom also served as the manager of Osborne Computer Corporation's software and publications departments during the first two years of that company's existence. Once in a while Thom is know to take potshots at the computer industry using the pseudonym Minnie Floppy, and is also sometimes coaxed into giving speeches at computer conferences. Otherwise, no one seems to know what Thom is up to, except that a truck arrives daily at his Palo Alto residence to deliver a supply of his favorite dependencies: a box of perforated, fanfold paper and a day's ration of caffeine-free, sugar-free RC100.

CONTENTS

Acknowledgments

This book would not have been possible without the help of a number of others. I'd like to thank all those who read the original manuscript: Frank Morton, Bob Briggs, Jim Wooley, Roger Chapman, Barbara Des Merais, and four anonymous, but extremely helpful, readers. Their fine eyes and excellent comments have made this book a bit closer to perfect.

I'd be remiss if I didn't thank Walt Bilofsky for this fine C/80 compiler, and Leor Zolman for his equally fine BDS c, both of which I used in preparing and checking many of the examples in CP/M-80. In addition, I used the Computer Innovations C86 compiler in checking results using MS-DOS.

And, of course, I must thank Dennis Ritchie for creating the original c language, and Dennis and Brian Kernighan for writing so eloquently about it, convincing so many of us that there was a better alternative.

Preface

This book is unique. While you can certainly read it from cover to cover, it is not to be read so much as to be used in day-to-day programming. I envision this book as an invaluable computer-side reference for anyone using the c language.

You will not learn how to program in c here. You will find a concise and (hopefully) complete definition of the language, with a strong bias toward programming practices that are not compiler or machine dependent.

The c language has evolved, leaping out of its traditional UNIX environment and permeating computer programming for all types of machines, big and small. As this evolution continues, this book will also evolve. Readers are encouraged to suggest improvements, modifications, corrections, and clarifications to this text for subsequent editions. Comments should be addressed to

Thom Hogan
The c Programmer's Handbook
Brady Communications Company, Inc.
Bowie, MD 20715

While I cannot promise to individually reply to all comments, rest assured comments both damning and praising are both read and appreciated.

—TH
Palo Alto, October 1983

Introduction

What This Book Is

This book provides the definitive desktop reference for anyone using the c. programming language. We assume you have already been introduced to the c language, are beginning to program in c, and must now grapple with understanding specific pieces of the language in the most efficient manner.

The title—*The c Programmer's Handbook*—gives some hint as to the organization of this book. Each topic is discussed separately, and there is a particular emphasis on clear organization and cross-referencing. The intention is to make this book a valuable computer-side reference.

If you're new to c, you will need something other than this book to get started. We suggest that you read *The c Programming Language* by Brian Kernighan and Dennis Ritchie (Prentice-Hall, 1978) to begin exploring the c language. Reading Kernighan and Ritchie isn't the easiest way to learn c, but the original definition of the language comes primarily from that particular work and the original c compiler written by Dennis Ritchie.

Other works attempt to fill in the gaps Kernighan and Ritchie left in their original volume. *c Notes* by C. T. Zahn (Yourdon Press, 1979) elaborated on the syntax and usage of c by someone other than those at Bell Laboratories, where c originated.

For almost three years, *The c Programming Language* and *c Notes* were the only readily available information on the c language. c grew in popularity during that period, and it became evident that more imformation about c was needed.

The c Puzzle Book by Alan Feuer (Prentice-Hall, 1982) is a unique work containing a series of questions about the c language for the reader to answer. Of course the answers are given, but the primary purpose of this book is to use self-learning techniques to teach c. Some elaboration of syntax and style is presented, drawn from Kernighan and Ritchie's original work.

Another unique book on c is Thomas Plum's *c Programming Standards and Guidelines* (Plum Hall, 1982), This book attempts to set down ironclad rules (and the reasons for them) to ensure that c programs written for one machine can be used on others. Thomas Plum also wrote *Learning to Program in c* (Plum Hall, 1983), an introduction to the language. This, and two other new books, *The c Primer* by Les Hancock and Morris Krieger (Byte Books, 1982), and *C Programming Guide* by Jack Purdum (Que, 1983), attempt to teach newcomers how to utilize the c language.

As this book went to production, two additional introductory books on c have appeared, while several more were announced. The two new books are *C Programming Tutor* by Wortman and Sidebottom (Brady, 1984), and *Programming in C* by Stephen Kochan (Hayden, 1983).

Each of these introductions has its relative weaknesses and merits; we'll leave it up to you to decide which one to read if you're new to c. No doubt many new books on c will have sprung up by the time you read this.

So where does this book fit in?

We have attempted to make this book unlike any other that has appeared on c. It is a distillation of information about c from all available sources.

This book is your reference work; your source for a specific answer to a specific question regarding c.

In a sense, this work is an attempt to define the c language. We collected all the information about c available, including the documentation for every c compiler we could identify. From this information the essential ingredients of the language were distilled. We hope this process will save you from having to make the same kind of exhaustive examination of the language in order to fully exploit its capabilities.

How to Use This Book

No compilation like this is ever complete, nor are compilations always perfect. The ultimate arbitrator of the c language will always be the c compiler you choose to work with. I've attempted to discuss major "disagreements" in implementation, but you may find others.

One requirement for using this book is that you be familiar with the c language in general. We've already briefly mentioned a number of books on c (and the bibliography in Appendix A should help you identify other sources of information), so you shouldn't have any problem gaining that general understanding requirement.

The manual that accompanies your c compiler is the second major source of information with which you'll need to be familiar. Unfortunately, it is here that a number of problems oftentimes creep in. Here are some areas where you might find differences between what is described in this book and what is described by your c compiler's manual:

- compiler-specific functions

- operating system requirements

- improper implementation of functions

- relaxing of compilation rules

Let's examine each of these a bit more thoroughly so you'll know the best approach to any idiosyncracies you may encounter. '

Compiler-specific functions are simple to explain: they are any function that is unique to the compiler you are using. One c compiler for microcomputers, for example, has PEEK and POKE functions, much like those found in most versions of the BASIC language. PEEK and POKE are unique to that compiler, having been invented (created?) specifically by the compiler's authors. In general, we recommend against using compiler-specific functions unless you know the program you are writing will never be moved ("ported," or "transported") to another computer system. Compiler-specific functions reduce the flexibility of your program, and may also teach you bad programming practices.

No truly compiler-specific functions are documented in this book (I've attempted to distill a "common" function library from the compilers available). Remember, with compiler-specific functions the compiler's authors are the authorities. You must attempt to find out from the compiler manual the reason the function was created, how it works, and the rules governing its use.

Operating system requirements pose a more troublesome problem. In many cases the c language "interacts" with the operating system; this is especially true of file operations. Obviously, if the c language you're using is implemented on an operating system other than the original (UNIX), there may be some major differences in how certain parts of the language work when compared with the original definition of c.

A good example of how the operating system changes the c language might be found in how a program is invoked. In UNIX, for example, you may type the name of the program, then any additional information—arguments, as Kernighan and Ritchie refer to them—needed by the program (each separated by a space):

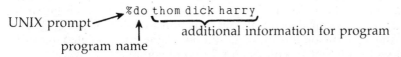

UNIX prompt⟶%do thom dick harry

program name   additional information for program

The c program then receives the three additional pieces of information, through the convention of argument passing to the MAIN function of the program:

```
main (argc, argv)
int argc;
char "argv;
```

where argc is the integer number of arguments that followed the program name and argv[] is an array of pointers to the actual arguments, which are themselves character strings.

Some operating systems don't allow "extra" information to be typed after a program name, thus the argument passing function of c cannot be used.

The same problem of possible non-implementation is possible with I/O redirection (the process of redirecting the output or input to or from devices other than the norm); many microcomputer operating systems don't allow such redirection.

This book documents some conventions that may not work under operating systems other than UNIX. We've tried to point out such cases and offer alternatives or more detail to show differences in operation.

The category of "improper implementation of functions" is less than exact in definition. Since no official standard for the c language exists, it is often difficult to tell whether or not an implementation of a particular function is adequately faithful to the definition of the c language.

Some of these problems are cosmetic. One c compiler named the "creat" function "create" to better facilitate program readability. The function worked exactly the same with either name, but the five-letter name is the historically correct one.

Other problems are not so obvious. Most often the problem lies with the differing machines being used for the different c compilers. A function on one machine may be working with 16-bit numbers, while another machine may use the same function with 32-bit numbers. The results, especially when you begin using the Boolean operators at the bit level, can be quite different in such cases.

There is no "good" method to avoid these often-minor-looking-but-major-consequences problems. For the most part, we have simply tried to elaborate on potential differences in functions and how these might affect your work. In those areas where bit sizes of data types might have an unwanted side effect on some compilers, we have pointed out this possibility. If you're using a UNIX version of c, you should investigate the utility program named lint; this performs some checking of a program's use of non-standard or idiosyncratic syntax.

The last of the potential problems you'll encounter in using this book is the relaxing of the compiler's rules. c is a very permissive compiler. In most cases a system of defaults goes into effect if you don't explicitly specify something.

A good example of this is the use of a passed value in a function. If you don't declare the data type, c normally assigns it an integer type. However, when you move the program from machine to machine, you'll begin to note that the program doesn't always function exactly the same. That's because the bit size of the integer number being manipulated may be different with different machines and different compilers.

Different c compilers have different methods for relaxing the rules and the assignment of default types and values. The first and best way to make sure you don't fall victim to this potential trap is to explicitly declare data types and leave the compiler no doubt as to your intent. This book assumes that attitude throughout; you'll find some shorthand tricks you may have learned are frowned upon or not even discussed here. Remember that data types are also in effect when declaring or using constants. The type casting operator (see page 94) can help when explicitly declaring constants.

Finally, you may wonder how it was decided which parts of the c language would be documented in this book and which would be left out. Some parts of the language are easily identified as being standard; others are not.

In general, we first identified the practical "core" of the c language. This includes the reserved words, operators, and compiler directives. To this we added those functions that appear in the UNIX 7 version of c, in Kernighan and Ritchie's work, and those that appear common to a number of different compilers. We have tried to keep the entries in this handbook restricted to only those that comprise the smallest accepted, yet still complete, set of c instructions.

Experienced c programmers will note the library functions are broken into groupings that may or may not match the library files they already use. Specifically, they are grouped into four categories:

Category (file name)

- Standard I/O functions (stdio.h)
- Standard string functions (string.h)
- Standard math functions (math.h)
- Other common functions

We have attempted to err on the side of compatibility and program portability when picking which functions to document: If the function is implemented differently by every c compiler, it shouldn't be part of what we would call the c standard. On the other hand, if the various implementations of a particular library function all tend to be the same, it is apparent that a quasi-standard exists and the function should be included here.

Table 1. Compatibility among c compilers.

Standard c (should be no problems)	Standard c (may vary with word sizes and compilers)	Should be checked against standard (likely to vary to some degree)
extern	char	all library functions
static	int	operating system characteristics
auto	long	I/O redirection
if	register	
else	# asm	
for	#endasm	
do	short	
while	structures	
switch	float	
case	double	
default	unsigned	
break	bit operators	
continue	enum	
goto	unions	
#define		
#undef		
#include		
#ifdef		
#ifndef		
#else		
#endif		
#line		
typedef		
main		
return		
sizeof		
symbolic representations		
most operators		

The task of determining whether a function is standard or non-standard is not without hazard. What most compilers regard as fact another may disregard entirely. We would discourage any c programmer from assuming that any predefined function exists in every compiler, including the ubiquitous printf.

To alleviate any confusion on the part of the reader as to what we think should be standard and what is questionably so, Table 1 shows where we would place each aspect of the c language.

Most of the instructions in Table 1 are generally regarded as the standard c instruction set. Despite this, there is actually little "safe ground" for writing portable programs. This is due to the variety of machines and compilers available. If in doubt, test each compiler you encounter to ascertain how it interprets a particular expression.

The Format Used to Describe Instructions

A similar format will be used for all c instructions presented in this book. This format is self-explanatory and generally looks like this:

NAME
   format
   purpose/definition
   rules governing usage
   defaults
   example usage
     preferred style
     alternate style (if any)
   exceptions
   returns

In the case of describing operators, this format is reduced to:

OPERATOR
   function
   example
   restrictions
   order
   priority level

You may find other minor differences in the format in each of the major sections, but these changes should be self-explanatory.

The instructions are also grouped into common areas so you can readily turn to the section you're interested in.

The major categories are:

general c program formatting
data types and classes
functions
operators and symbolic representations
compiler directives
control structures
I/O library functions
string library functions
math library functions
other library functions

The first section, general program formatting concerns, is a discussion of how the elements of a c program are normally arranged. The formatting section is followed by a section on defining variables and data structures, information pertaining to data types and classes, and how to specify them.

How functions are created and the components of functions comes next. Operators and arithmetic expressions follow; you might be familiar with these by the names of unary and binary operations. The symbolic representations unique to c, such as how to denote a number as hex, decimal, or octal, are discussed at the end of the operators section.

These four sections represent the gritty "detail" of the c language, and you'll probably find yourself referring to them more often than the rest. You might say this first half of the reference deals primarily with telling c WHAT you can do with the various components.

The next portion of the reference section is mainly devoted to telling the c compiler WHEN to do WHAT and HOW. It starts with compiler directives then moves to control structures. Compiler directives are instructions to be carried out before the actual compilation process. Control structures are simply instructions pertaining to the direction or redirection of program control. It is here you'll find the loops and case testing capabilities of c.

Finally, there is a library of functions commonly found with most c compilers.

You'll also find a number of useful appendices at the back of the book, including a bibliography, an ASCII coding chart in several number bases, some common function and definition files, and other general information that doesn't fit into the main body of this book. Also included is a detailed index so you can look up all mentions of a specific c keyword or function.

Some Definitions

Before going on, let's elaborate on the shorthand nomenclature used in FORMAT section of each reference. Here's an example of a FORMAT section you'll encounter (this one is for the keyword "char"):

FORMAT

```
char name;
char name-list;
class char name;
class char name-list;
```

Obviously, the "char" in each of the above formatting examples represents the c language item being described. Note that this material is underlined; underlined characters must appear in your program exactly as they appear in the example (in the same order, using the same spelling, same case, same punctuation, and so on).

The other words are a form of shorthand, for which you substitute another piece of information. For example, "name" in the above example means you should substitute a valid variable (or function) name in place of the word "name." Instead of typing

```
char name;
```

in your program, you should type something like

```
char my_variable;
```

where "my_variable" is a name you use within your program.

Here's a complete list of what the shorthand used in the FORMAT sections means, and what you should substitute in place of each:

arguments   Substitute a list of arguments, normally a list of variable names, each separated by a comma.

buffer   Substitute a pointer to a usable memory location, or an expression that reduces to a memory location.

character   Substitute a char type data value (or char type variable name), or an expression that reduces to a char type data value.

class   Substitute a valid data storage class (auto, static, extern, register).

commentary   Substitute any program comments.

constant   Substitute a constant value or a constant name.

constant-expression   Substitute a constant or an expression that reduces to a constant.

conversion-string   Substitute a valid scanf or printf conversion string (see Appendix E).

expression   Substitute a valid c expression. This includes variable names, functions, operators, and so on.

filename   Substitute a valid filename for your particular operating system (this includes both name and type for CP/M systems, and pipes for UNIX systems).

file pointer   Substitute a file pointer (as returned from a fopen statement).

float   Substitute a double or float type data value (or a double or float variable name), or an expression that reduces to a double or float type data value.

formatting-string   Substitute a valid printf formatting string (see Appendix E).

function-name   Substitute a valid function name (including the parentheses representing the argument portion of the function call).

identifier   Substitute an uppercase name that otherwise conforms to c naming conventions (see page 2).

initialization   Substitute a c statement to be executed before the loop is entered; this statement is optional.

incrementation   Substitute a c statement to be executed after each iteration of the loop; this statement is optional.

integer   Substitute an int type data value (or int type variable name), or an expression that reduces to an int type data value.

label   Substitute a name that is used to refer to a place within the program (see goto for a detailed explanation, page 128).

mode   Substitute a valid file mode (0 for reading, 1 for writing, or 2 for reading and writing).

name Substitute a valid variable or function name (see page 2 for naming conventions). Remember, function names include the argument parentheses immediately following the actual name.

name-list Substitute a valid series (list) of variable names, each separated by a comma (again, see page 2 for naming conventions).

number Substitute an integer value (or expression that reduces to an integer value) that represents a number.

offset Substitute an integer value (or expression that reduces to an integer value) that represents a number of bytes.

origin Substitute an integer value (or expression that reduces to an integer value) that represents a particular place (counted by bytes) within a file.

pointer Substitute a pointer value (or an expression that reduces to a pointer value).

size Substitute an integer value (or expression that reduces to an integer value) that represents a size (in bytes).

statement Substitute any valid c statement, or substitute a series of valid c statements enclosed in braces ({})

storage-string Substitute a pointer to a string to be used for storage.

string Substitute a pointer to a string, or an explicitly declared string.

struct-name Same as "name"; see above. The reason for making a distinction between name and struct-name is so you don't accidentally substitute a variable or function name for a structure name.

test Substitute a valid c statement, normally testing a value or expression for equivalence to TRUE or FALSE, to be used during each iteration of a loop to check for completion.

type Substitute a valid data type (int, double, float, char, long, unsigned, short).

union-name Same as "name"; see above. The reason for making a distinction between name and union-name is so you don't accidentally substitute a variable or function name for a union name.

value Substitute the actual value to be used for data; it must match the data type in which it is to be stored.

variable-name Same as "name"; see above. The reason for making a distinction between name and variable-name is so you don't accidentally substitute a function name for a variable name.

1

Program Format and General Defaults

Components of a c Program

The following are the basic ingredients of a c program:

1. **Names (or identifiers).** Variables and functions are referred to by programmer-selected names. Most compilers allow upper and lowercase letters, numbers (if not the first character) and the underline character to be used in creating names. Names cannot be reserved words (see page 3 for a list of reserved words). Only the first six characters of a name are read by some c compilers, so the first six characters of each name must be unique. More characters may be entered, but the compiler might not use them in distinguishing between names.

   The original UNIX compiler, for instance, allows eight characters in a name, while the current version (7) allows an unlimited number of characters. For portability of programs, it is suggested you make sure the first six characters are always unique, no matter what length names you choose to use. In addition, always use the same trailing characters (those after the initial, required-to-be unique ones) for names you expect to be treated the same, even if your current cc npiler ignores these trailing characters. You may find in a later update of your own compiler, that names you expected to be the same are now treated differently.

2. **Constants.** Constants are data values that do not change. Constants can be designated in any of the following ways:

constant type	how specified
int (in decimal)	Type the number.
int (in octal)	Type 0 (zero), then the number.
int (in hexadecimal)	Type 0x (zero, x), then the number.
long	Type an l (lowercase "L") after the number.
char	Enclose the character in single quotes ('). Some specific special characters are defined by preceding them with a backslash (\). See the section of symbolic representations (page 95) for details on these characters.
string	Enclose the character(s) in double quotes ("). Strings are always an array of char type data, and have the storage class of static.
float or **double**	Type the number and include a decimal point in it. A floating point number may be expressed in exponential notation by including an E (or e) and an optionally signed integer exponent.

3. **Whitespace.** c compilers allow the programmer to "format" program code using whitespace characters almost at will. Certain exceptions apply to this rule (such as functions, where a space cannot appear between the function name and its argument list) and are discussed in the appropriate sections later in this book. Whitespace characters are:

name	ASCII value (in hex)	representation
blank or space	20	\040
backspace	08	\b
horizontal tab	09	\t
vertical tab	0B	\v
form feed	0C	\f
newline	0A	\n
carriage return	0D	\r

4. **Separators** (or punctuation). Certain punctuation characters are regarded by c as having specific syntactical meanings.

character	meaning
;	End of a c statement.
{	Start of a block of statements that should be considered as a single statement for program control purposes.
}	End of a block of statements.
(	Used to force priority of the enclosed expression to a higher level than that of any expression external to the parentheses, or used to contain a function argument list.
)	Ends forced priority of the enclosed expression, or denotes end of a function argument list.
[]	Used to denote an array, see page 14 for more details.

5. **Operators.** See Section 4 on Operators, page 47, for a complete description.

6. **Keywords.** The control statements c automatically recognizes. See Sections 5 and 6, on Compiler Directives and Control Statements, beginning on page 97 for complete descriptions of these elements. The following is a complete list of the keywords c recognizes:

auto	break	case	char
continue	default	do	double
else	entry*	enum*	extern
float	for	goto	if
int	long	register	return
sizeof	short	static	struct
switch	typedef	union	unsigned
while	void*		

*may not be in all UNIX compilers

Some compilers also consider the following as keywords:
asm   fortran

Creating a c Program

The following are the steps normally used in creating a c program:

step	uses	input	output
create	editor	terminal	source code file
preprocess	cc (or sometimes cpp)	source code file	c code file
compile	cc2	c code file	assembly language file
check (optional)	lint	source code file	listing with warnings
assemble	as (sometimes asm or masm)	assembly language file	object code file
link	link	object code file	a.out (program name)
run	a.out (or program name)	program file	

Portions of this process may be different under operating systems other than UNIX and compilers other than the UNIX version 7 compiler (see Appendix C). Some portions of the process may not be seen by the user. They are performed automatically by computer after the preprocessor is started; to the user it may appear as if several of the above steps were combined.

The following is an annotated session that illustrates the above steps, using CP/M-80 and the popular BDS c compiler. The program used as an example is a slightly modified version of the Sieve of Eratosthenes benchmark written by Jim & Gary Gilbreath and published in the January 1983 *Byte* magazine.

CP/M-80 and BDS c Example

```
A>ed bench.c
*i
/*
 * BENCH.C
 *
 * A program to compute prime numbers using the Sieve of
 * Eratosthenes method. Program originally appeared in
 * Byte magazine, January 1983 issue, written by Jim and
 * Gary Gilbreath. Modifications and comments by Thom
 * Hogan.
 *
 */
```

```c
#include <stdio.h>

#define SIZE    8190    /* number of numbers to test      */
#define NTIMES  10      /* number of times to run benchmark */
#define FALSE   0       /* logical false condition        */
#define TRUE    !FALSE  /* logical true condition         */

char flag[SIZE + 1];    /* array to hold primes           */

main()
{
        int i, j, k, count, prime;

        printf("%d iterations\n",NTIMES);
        for(i = 1; i <= NTIMES; i++)
        {
                count = 0;                      /* prime counter */
                for(j = 0; j <= SIZE; j++)
                        flag[j] = TRUE;  /* set all flags true */
                for(j = 0; j <= SIZE; j++)
                {
                        if(flag[j])     /* flag[j] is TRUE */
                        {
                                prime = j + j + 3; /* twice index + 3 */
                                printf("\n%d is prime",prime);
                                for(k = j + prime; k <= SIZE; k += prime)
                                        flag[k] = FALSE;
                                count++
                        } /* end if */
                } /* end for(j */
        } /* end for (i */
        printf("%d primes found.\n",count);
        exit(0);
} /* end main */
^Z
*e

A>cc bench
BD Software c Compiler v1.50a (part I)
33k elbowroom

A>cc2 bench
BD Software c Compiler v1.50 (part II)
30k to spare

A>clink bench
BD Software c linker v1.50
Linkage complete
41k left over

A>bench
10 iterations
3 is prime
5 is prime
7 is prime
  . . .
  . . .
1899 primes found.

A>
```

Here is the same annotated session, but using UNIX c.

UNIX Version 7 Example

```
$ ed bench.c
?bench.c
a
/*
 *BENCH.C
 *
 * A program to compute prime numbers using the Sieve of
 * Eratosthenes method. Program originally appeared in
 * Byte magazine, January 1983 issue, written by Jim and
 * Gary Gilbreath. Modifications and comments by Thom
 * Hogan.
 *
 */

#include <stdio.h>

#define SIZE    8190    /* number of numbers to test        */
#define NTIMES  10      /* number of times to run benchmark */
#define FALSE   0       /* logical false condition          */
#define TRUE    !FALSE  /* logical true condition           */

char flag[SIZE + 1];    /* array to hold primes             */

main()
{
        int     i, j, k, count, prime;

        printf("%d iterations\n",NTIMES);
        for(i = 1; i <= NTIMES; i++)
        {
                count = 0;              /* prime counter */
                for(j = 0; j <= SIZE; j++)
                        flag[j] = TRUE; /* set all flags true */
                for(j = 0; j <= SIZE; j++)
                {
                        if(flag[j])       /* flag[j] is TRUE */
                        {
                        prime = j + j + 3; /* twice index + 3 */
                        printf("\n%d is prime",prime);
                        for(k = j + prime; k <= SIZE; k += prime
                        flag[k] = FALSE;
                        count++
                        /* end if */
                } /* end for(j */
        } /* end for (i */
        printf("%d primes found.\n",count);
        exit(0);
} /* end main */
^D
w
q

$ cc bench.c

$ a.out
10 iterations
3 is prime
5 is prime
```

```
7 is prime
  . . .
  . . .
1899 primes found.

$
```

Program Format

There are numerous ways to format a c program. c is generally a permissive compiler; it doesn't care about white spaces, carriage returns, and other formatting materials. It simply looks at the syntax of the actual code and does its job accordingly.

Because of this formatting flexibility, a number of programming format styles are used by c programmers. Kernighan and Ritchie, for example, use a programming style that tends to compact the source code. This makes the program a bit less readable than it could be.

The programming format suggested here is simple to follow, leads to very readable c code, and appears to be preferred by most non-Bell Laboratories c programmers. Here are the rules for using this format.

1. All subordinate lines should be tabbed in, preferably only four spaces (but eight spaces is acceptable). The only exception to this rule is preprocessor commands (those beginning with a # sign), which should always be at the lefthand margin; some compilers require this.

   A subordinate line is defined as any line whose execution is dependent upon a condition being met in a previous one, or whenever a group of statements is combined into a block using braces ({ }). For example:

```
if ((c = getchar()) != EOF)    /* commanding line */
        putchar(c);            /* subordinate line */
else                           /* commanding line */
        exit();                /* subordinate line */
```

   Tabbing in this manner allows the program reader to quickly see relationships between the various statements, especially in control structures.

   The definition given above for subordinate lines is not the only one possible. If you use a different definition, make sure your rules are clearly expressed and you are unfailingly consistent in applying them.

2. Any "null" statement (one which does nothing, as in the case of the semicolon all by itself), should be on a line of its own. Example:

```
for (i = 0; i <= 9; ++i)
    ;                        /* null statement */
```

   Another alternative is to use #define to create a named null statement, like this:

```
#define null_statement
  . . .
  . . .
for (i=0; i <= 9; ++i)
    null_statement;
```

3. The general structure of the program should be as follows:

> 0. comment identifying program
> 1. files to be included into source code (#includes)
> 2. definitions (#defines)
> 3. external variable declarations (externs)
> 4. function main
> 5. defined functions, preferably ordered in some logical fashion (alphabetical, hierarchical, calling order, etc.)

A blank line should appear between each of the above items. For the format used in defining functions, see the section on functions, page 41.

4. Braces ({ and }) should get a line of their own, at the same indentation level as the controlling statement they relate to. The statements appearing between braces should be indented, as explained in rule #1 above. The exception to this is in array initialization, which should follow the conventional practice described on page 15. For example:

```
while ( ( c = getchar() ) != EOF )
{
        do1();
        do2();
}
```

5. Unless specifically prohibited in the description of a c keyword or function later in this book, the programmer should use whitespace liberally so one can easily see the relationships between component parts. It is not necessary to try to conserve spaces; the c compiler will strip them out during compilation (except, of course, inside strings set in quotes).

General Defaults

The following standard compiler defaults should be considered when creating a c program:

1. Functions with undeclared types are considered to be of type (signed) int.

2. Variables must be explicity declared as to their type (char, int, and so on).

3. Variables not explicitly declared in a particular storage class (*i.e.*, static, register, and so forth), are created as storage class auto within a function definition; otherwise, they are created with a storage class of extern.

4. c does not necessarily guarantee the order of evaluation of the components in a statement (other than the precedence and order of operators). Do not rely upon the order in which the components of a statement are evaluated.

5. c does not check for variable overflow.

6. Variables declared without an initializer (an = followed by a constant) contain garbage (unreliable information) until initialized. Note: The UNIX versions of c automatically default a value of zero to globally-defined variables, and a great deal of code has been written that depends upon this action. Nevertheless, you should not rely upon this when programming in c.

7. Strings are automatically an array of characters with a storage class of static.

8. In initializing arrays using an initializer list, any non-used elements are set to zero. For example:

```
int array[2][2] = {1}, {2};
```

yields the following initial values:

```
array[0][0] = 1
array[0][1] = 2
array[1][0] = 0
array[0][1] = 0
```

Individual compilers may add to this list of defaults. Check your compiler's reference manual for more details.

2

Data Types and Storage Classes

Naming Restrictions

The following rules apply to the naming of variables:

1. Variable names may be upper or lowercase letters and include numbers (after the first letter) or the underline character. Upper and lowercase letters are regarded as being different, thus NAME, Name, and name are considered different variable names in c. Most experienced c programmers use only lowercase variable names and reserve uppercase names for constants and parameters (e.g., #define PI 3.1415).

2. Keywords may not be used as a variable name in c. Keywords may be contained within a variable name, however (life is a valid name, despite the fact it contains the keyword if). A list of keywords appears on page 3. Keywords consist only of lowercase letters; IF is a valid variable name.

3. Short (one character) names are often used by c programmers for temporary or unimportant counter variables, with the following common meanings:

variable name	variable type/meaning
c	char type variable
d	double type variable
i	
j	int type variables used for counting
k	
n	counter variable
p	
q	pointer variables
s	variable containing a string
x	
y	float type variables
z	

Careless use of these naming conventions can result in difficult to understand (and maintain) program code.

4. Variable names should be meaningful (i.e., the casual reader of the program code should be able to understand what is stored in the variable from its name) and should have the first six characters distinct, even though many compilers use the first eight characters for identification purposes. The latest UNIX compiler allows even longer names, but, for portability purposes, the first six characters of a name should always be made unique, if possible.

5. Some experienced c programmers alphabetize variables within type declarations, making it easier to find a particular variable name when scanning the code.

Initialization

The rules regarding the initialization of variables and the placement of values in variables are as follows.

1. Newer c compilers allow initializing a value for a variable at declaration time in the following form:

   ```
   type name = value;
   ```

   Older style c compilers initialize values in a declaration as follows:

   ```
   type name value;
   ```

   (Code written for these older compilers may require changing before it will correctly compile on most versions of c.)

2. If a variable counts something, it is common practice to initialize it to its starting value in the variable's declaration statement. This is to ensure the variable always has a proper value in it, even if it is only zero. Be careful of the situation in which you re-enter a loop and do not reinitialize the counting variable.

   ```
   int counter = 1;          /* this is bad code! */
   ...
   for(;counter = 10; ++counter)
       do_something();
   ```

   should be:

   ```
   int counter;
   ...
   for(counter = 1;counter = 10; ++counter)
           do_something();
   ```

   This is an overly simple and not very realistic example. The point should be obvious: do not count on an initializer in a variable declaration to insure that a variable used to control a loop has a proper value before entering the loop.

3. Variables usually contain garbage (nonsensical information) until initialized (see page 31 for the exception). Static and external variables not initialized are guaranteed to start off with an initial value of zero.

4. Avoid initializing variables in header files that are brought into the source code using the #include directive, since ownership and scope (extent of usage) of these variables may be in question on some c compilers.

5. Automatic variables (storage class auto) may be initialized, but remember the memory is not allocated until run-time. Automatic variables are initialized each time a function containing them is invoked.

6. Although not an ironclad rule, when initializing structures, unions, and arrays with values, you should format the statement with a single dimension (structure) per line:

```
type name = {one dimension,
            two dimensions,
            three dimensions,
                 .
                 .
                 .
            n dimensions};
```

Adhering to this style makes the internal structure obvious to the casual program reader.

Arrays

The following rules apply to the declaration and use of arrays:

1. Arrays are declared and identified by using square brackets ([and]) immediately after the variable name (no whitespace normally appears between the name and the brackets, even though some c compilers allow it). A number appearing within the brackets refers to the number of elements in the array if used in a declaration statement (int array[6]; declares a six-element array). Elsewhere it indicates the element of the array to use (the assignment statement array[5] = b; assigns the value of b to the sixth element in the variable array, since elements are counted from zero after initialization; see point 3 below).

2. Elements of an array can be of any data type, but all elements in an array must be of the same data type. In other words, you may have an array of all char type elements, all int type elements, and so on, but not one that intermixes char and int type elements (see union, page 37, for an alternative to arrays that allows different type elements).

3. One source of confusion with arrays is that a number within the brackets ([6]) can mean one of two different things, depending upon context. When an array is declared, the number within the brackets refers to the number of elements to reserve space for, and it is counted starting with 1. Example:

   ```
   int array[6];      /* indicates a six-element array */
   ```

   When arrays are used in statements other than declaration (initialization) statements, the number in the brackets is counted starting with 0 (zero). Example:

   ```
   array[5] = 4;      /* sets the sixth element of
                         the array to a value of 4 */
   ```

   The reason for this apparent discrepancy has to do with c's use of pointers and the manner in which pointers are incremented.

   &array[0] points to the beginning of the storage area for an array.

   &array[1] points to the beginning of the storage area for an array plus an incrementation of one element.

All array counts and element numbers must be integers.

4. Compilers vary on the number of dimensions an array may have; five is a common limit.

5. You must specifically state how many elements are in an array when it is first declared by enclosing a number in the brackets, or by having an initialization list from which c can generate a count of elements. Initialization of values (optional), is done as follows:

```
type name[elements] = {value list;}
```

with each value in the list separated by a comma. The number of elements in the declaration should match the number of values in the value list. If the number of elements is greater than the number of values, the compiler's default initializations result. If the number of values is greater than the number of elements, an error is usually generated at compile time. The number of elements need not be specified if the compiler can figure it out from the initialization list. Initialization of an array is only allowed if the storage class is extern or static; auto storage class arrays may not be initialized at declaration time.

6. Multi-dimensional arrays are declared as follows:

```
type name[elements][elements];       /* two dimensions */
type name[elements][elements][elements];   /* three dimensions
```

and so on. Elements are stored in such a way that, if they are accessed in the order in which they are stored, the rightmost dimension varies fastest.

7. Array elements are stored in sequential locations. Pointers to arrays automatically are scaled for the size of the array's data type. Incrementing an array pointer always results in the pointer pointing to the next element, not necessarily the next memory location.

8. When an array name is used by itself (after declaration), it is assumed to stand for the address of the first element in the array. Thus

```
array;
```

is the equivalent of

```
&array[0];
```

9. Strings are special one-dimensional arrays of characters terminated by a null (\0). A string is represented by a series of characters enclosed in double quotes (") and must be of type char. The null character at the end of the array is added automatically by the c compiler; you type

```
array[] = "string";
```

and not

```
array[] = "string\0";
```

NOTE: You must allow space for the extra character (the \0). In the above example, array[] contains *seven* characters, not the six you might at first assume.

10. When an array is passed as an argument to a function, the address of the first element is passed, not the value. Array variables are not necessarily private to a function as other arguments normally are.

Pointers

Pointers are often confusing to newcomers. Some of the confusion results from the shorthand method c uses to indicate pointers. Also confusing is the distinction between a variable containing an address rather than a value. Consider the following sequence of statements:

```
int a, *b, c;
a = 1;          /* a's value is 1                    */
b = &a;         /* b's value is the address of a    */
c = *b;         /* c's value is the value at the
                   address pointed to by b           */
```

Here's what happened internally when this code was executed.

name	location	contents
a	x	1
*b	x + 2	x
c	x + 4	1

The first assignment, a = 1, is easy to understand; the value stored in variable a is now 1. The second assignment, b = &a, results in the storage of the address (location) of variable a as the contents in variable b (note we had to declare b as a pointer—*b in the int statement—because it was going to be used to store an address); think of the & sign meaning "address of." The third assignment, c = *b, tells the compiler to store in variable c the value at the address contained in b; you think of the * sign as meaning "value at address contained in."

Another aspect of pointers not obvious to newcomers is the way they are incremented. A pointer variable (a variable whose contents point to the contents of another variable, like *b in the above example) always has a type: a pointer to an int, a pointer to a char, and so on. This distinction is important, since the word length (in bits) of different data types varies. An int is often 16 bits, for instance. Consider the following:

```
int a, *b, c;
a = 1;
b = &a;
b++;
c = *b;
b--;
c = *b;
```

Here's what happens internally as this sequence was executed.

statement	variable a at location x	variable b at location x + 2	variable c at location x + 4
1. int a, *b, c	?*	?*	?*
2. a = 1;	1	?*	?*
3. b = &a;	1	x	?*
4. b++;	1	x + 2	?*
5. c = *b;	1	x + 2	x + 2**
6. b--;	1	x	x + 2
7. c = *b;	1	x	1

*Different compilers will have differing contents after the variable declaration statement.

**Note: c ends up with the same value as b in this example by coincidence, since b happens to point at itself; notice what happens in steps 6 and 7.

auto

Name

auto

Format

```
auto type name;
auto type name-list;
```

Purpose

The auto keyword is used to declare a storage class of automatic for a variable.

Usage Rules

1. Automatic storage class means memory is not reserved for the variable in question, and c dynamically allocates memory for the variable when needed.

2. The content of the named variable is garbage until a value has been assigned to it, unless an initializer is provided.

3. An automatic variable is local to the function in which it is declared.

4. Any data type variable may be declared using the auto storage class.

5. Variable names in a "name-list" are separated by commas.

6. Other storage classes (static, extern, register, and typedef) may not appear in a declaration that includes auto.

Defaults

If no storage class is specified in a variable declaration within a function, it is assumed to be auto(matic).

Example

Sample usage:

```
auto int number;
number = 1;
```

Exceptions

None.

Returns

Not applicable.

char

Name

char

Format

```
char name;
char name-list;
class char name;
class char name-list;
```

Purpose

The char variable data type is used to tell the compiler you are dealing
with a single character of information.

Usage Rules

1. The char type variable is assumed to be an 8-bit (or more) memory
   location. The char type variable normally uses the most significant bit
   as a sign; integer values from -128 to 127 (representing characters) may
   be stored in this type of variable. Some compilers may not allow the
   sign, restricting values to zero through 127. In general, do not use char
   type variables for storing numeric values unless those values directly
   represent characters.

2. A char type variable should not contain more than one character, even
   if the bit length is longer than 8. Use strings for multi-character data
   values. Some compilers allow multiple char constants (char might contain 16 bits, enough for two ASCII characters, for example). Such use
   should be avoided since it is not portable to other compilers.

3. Char type variables are easily (and often) converted to signed integer
   variables in most operations.

4. Char type values are initialized by enclosing a character in single quotes
   ('), as in

   ```
   character = 'a';
   ```

5. Variable names in a name-list are separated by commas:
   ```
   char name1, name2, name3;
   ```

Defaults

None.

Example

Sample uses:

```
char letter;
letter = 'a';
```

char

```
char *point;
point = "Hello reader.";
```

Exceptions

None.

Returns

Not applicable.

double

Name

double

Format

```
double name;
double name-list;
class double name;
class double name-list;
```

Purpose

The double keyword is used to declare a data type of double-precision, floating point number for the named variable.

Usage Rules

1. c compilers normally store double numbers as 64 bits, with 14 digits of precision.

2. Double numbers are generally stored in the following internal memory format:

   sign
   14 digits, usually encoded to conserve space
   exponent

3. Rounding errors may occur when using double numbers.

4. Variable names in a name-list are separated by commas:

   ```
   double name1, name2, name3;
   ```

Defaults

None.

Example

Sample use:

```
double pleasure;
pleasure = 3.14159;
```

Exceptions

Compilers differ on the exact internal memory usage for double numbers, although most do have 14 digits of precision for double numbers.

Returns

Not applicable.

extern

Name

extern

Format

```
extern type name;
extern type name-list;
```

Purpose

The extern storage class keyword directs that the named variable(s) already exist, are global in nature (i.e., available to other functions), and are defined elsewhere.

Usage Rules

1. Variables declared as being extern are defined outside of the current function. If a conflict in variable names arises between an extern and a local variable, the local variable is used within a function.

2. Values for extern declared variables are kept in memory at all times, as opposed to the transient nature of variables of the auto class.

3. Any function that uses an external variable (one defined before or outside of function main) should explicitly declare the variable name as being extern within the function. Otherwise external variables must be defined prior to the function(s) in which they're used.

4. External variables should be avoided whenever possible, since they take up memory and names, and functions that use them are not necessarily portable. External variables are properly used when compiling a program in segments, and when the functions within these various segments need to share global variables.

5. Other class types (static, auto, register, and typedef) may not appear in a declaration that includes extern.

6. The type used with an extern declaration must match other declarations for the variable or unpredictable results will be obtained.

Defaults

None.

Example

Sample use:

```
int number = 1;      /* defined externally */
main()
{
    extern int number; /* explicitly declared for function */
    something();
}
```

extern

Possible alternate use:

```
#define COMMON int number
COMMON = 1;
main( )
{
    extern COMMON;
    something( );
}
```

extern

Exceptions

None.

Returns

Not applicable.

FILE

Name

FILE

Format

FILE name;

Purpose

The FILE data type is sometimes a single int that contains a file number, but more often is a structure used to declare all the pertinent variables needed for file access (mode, buffer location, buffer size, and so on).

Usage Rules

1. The definition for FILE on a particular system is usually included in the header file, stdio.h. Since FILE is often a structure, several variables (members) are usually declared by this data type.

2. Programmers use the derived type of FILE as an easier method of keeping track of all the information relating to the access of one particular file.

3. FILE is almost always spelled in capital letters.

Defaults

None.

Example

Highly compiler specific, check your manual for an example, if implemented. To include the definition for FILE in your program, use

```
#include <stdio.h>
```

Exceptions

FILE is not defined by the compiler. The programmer must define it using typedef (or #define) or get its definition from a stdio.h file. FILE is highly compiler and operating system dependent.

Returns

Not applicable.

float

Name

float

Format

```
float name;
float name-list;
class float name;
class float name-list;
```

Purpose

The float keyword declares a single-precision, floating point variable.

Usage Rules

1. Floats are typically stored as 32-bit numbers with 6 digits of precision.

2. The normal storage method consists of the following components, in this order:

   sign
   6 digits, normally encoded to conserve space
   exponent

3. A float may contain a value that has a decimal point and a value after the decimal point.

4. Great care should be exercised in using variables of the float type, since rounding errors can easily accumulate.

5. Each variable name in a variable list should be separated by a comma:

   ```
   float name1, name2, name3;
   ```

Defaults

None.

Example

Sample usage:

```
float pie;
pie = 3.14159;
```

Exceptions

None.

Returns

Not applicable.

int

Name

int

Format

```
int name;
int name-list;
class int name;
class int name-list;
```

Purpose

The int keyword is used to declare variables of an integer-only type.

Usage Rules

1. Most common length for int variables is 16 bits, with 32 bits being common on mainframes and larger minicomputers.

2. Unless the keyword "unsigned" is present, integers are considered to be signed (positive or negative) values. With 16-bit integers, the range of values that may be stored is from -32768 to 32767. The high-order bit is considered to be the sign bit.

3. Integers are whole numbers only. For example, no fractional part appears after decimal points when an int type variable is converted to floating point.

Defaults

Int is the default type for variables.

Example

Sample use:

```
int holenum;
holenum = 30;
```

Exceptions

Some programmers use a #define to make the bit size of integer variables obvious to anyone reading the program:

```
#define SIZE16 int
 . . .
SIZE16 variable;
```

Returns

Not applicable.

long

Name

long

Format

```
long name;
long name-list;
long type name;
long type name-list;
class long name;
class long name-list;
class long type name;
class long type name-list;
```

Purpose

The long keyword is a modifier that declares variables to be stored in twice the space as normal.

Usage Rules

1. Long-type variables that are integers normally hold 32 bits of information (or more—almost always twice the length of type short), although some microcomputer compilers make long the same as int (16 bits). The range of integer numbers that may be stored in 32 bits is from -2,147,483,648 to 2,147,483,647.

2. Long-type variables that are floating point are the same as type double.

Defaults

If no type is specified, a variable type of int is assumed.

Example

Sample use:

```
long int huey;
huey = 324566;

long float ivory;
ivory = 672.19586;
```

Exceptions

Some variable types may not be changed by some compilers by using the long modifier.

Returns

Not applicable.

register

Name

register

Format

```
register type name;
register type name-list;
```

Purpose

The register class of variables is stored in the central processor's internal registers, when possible, to speed up calculations with often-used variables.

Usage Rules

1. The internal registers of the central processor must be large enough to hold the variable's value. If not, even though declared as class register, the variable will revert to class auto. Some types of variables cannot be stored in registers: structures, unions, and arrays.

2. An internal register must be free at the time the register declaration is made. If not, even though declared as class register, the variable will revert to class auto.

3. You cannot get the address of a register variable (preceding the variable name with an & sign, as in **&name,** doesn't work with register variables).

4. Register-class variables are local to the function that declares them.

5. Many programmers avoid register variable use, since the benefit of using them is machine-specific. Obviously, using c to program an operating system or other low-level driver often benefits from use of register variables. The decision to use register variables should be made considering the level at which you are programming and the implied trade-off between speed and portability.

6. Other class types (static, extern, auto, and typedef) may not appear in a declaration that includes register.

Defaults

None.

Example

Sample use:

```
register int cash;
cash = received - change + startamt;
```

register

Exceptions

A register must be free. The register must be big enough to store the result. Some compilers restrict register variables to type int or char, due to the size of the registers available. Some compilers do not use actual registers for register-class variables, but manipulate stack, memory, or alternate register sets for register variable use. Some compilers won't place certain variable types in registers because it would offer no speed advantage (char-type variables on machines with 32-bit or larger registers, for example).

Register is highly machine and compiler specific. On some machines, using the address of what you have declared to be a register variable results in an error if a register was actually assigned; if no error occurs, a register was not assigned, the variable was converted to a type of auto.

register

Returns

Not applicable.

short

Name

short

Format

```
short name;
short name-list;
short type name;
short type name-list;
```

Purpose

The short keyword is a modifier used to declare a particular int type variable as using half the space as is normal.

Usage Rules

1. Most compilers make short int the same length (in bits) as int (generally 16 bits). Only on larger machines (typically with 32 bit ints) are short integers stored in less space than normal integers. Therefore, the rules for using short variables are basically the same as for those using type int.

2. Some compilers may allow short to be used with types other than int, but this is not standard.

Defaults

If no variable type is declared, int is assumed.

Example

Sample use:

```
short people;
people = 0;      /* or 99 if you happen
                    to be short! */
```

Exceptions

Most compilers do not allow short to be used with any type other than int. Most compilers for smaller computers do not actually use less storage space for short variables.

Returns

Not applicable.

static

Name

static

Format

```
static type name;
static type name-list;
static type name = value;
extern static type name;
extern static type name-list;
extern static type name = value;
```

Purpose

The static class of variable is similar to the auto class, but the value is retained when the function is completed, and that value is available the next time the function is invoked.

Usage Rules

1. Static class variables are local to the function in which they are defined, unless they are declared externally.

2. An initial value is assigned to a static variable at compilation time, meaning that space is assigned and an initial value stored there. This is as opposed to the auto class variable, whose value and space are assigned at run time, and only when the variable is active (as within a function that declares it).

3. Static class variables are best avoided, if possible, since they permanently take up memory space and often result in the same sort of overuse as the goto statement (static variables can make program code less easily understood). On the other hand, some types of programming require that information be kept in memory permanently. Since static variables defined outside a function are shared by all functions in a file, they are often used to keep a line count or other semi-global variable, where all functions can access the data. Use static variables only if you can justify your reason for doing so; otherwise avoid them.

4. Other class types (register, extern, auto, and typedef) may not appear in a declaration that includes static.

Defaults

If no initialization appears, the initial value of a static class variable is set to zero (0).

Example

Sample use:

```
static char noise = 'T';
```

static

Exceptions

None.

Returns

Not applicable.

struct

Name

struct

Format

```
struct struct-name {member-declaration-list};
struct struct-name {member-declaration-list}; variable-
name;
struct struct-name {member-declaration-list}; variable-name
= value;
struct struct-name variable-name;
```

Purpose

The struct specification of variable declares a group of related variables to be referred to by one structure (group) name.

Usage Rules

1. The closing semicolon after the closing curly bracket (}) must be present, even though this may not seem to coincide with some other parts of c syntax.

2. The member-declaration-list is a set of variable declarations, one for each member of the group of variables to be contained in the structure.

3. Structures can be declared or defined as follows. Struct can be used to allocate space when a variable-name is used in the statement. This is called a structure declaration. Otherwise struct does not allocate space. When no variable-name is declared, struct defines only the form of the structure, which may be used later to define a variable (and thus allocated space). This is called a structure definition.

   Applying an existing structure definition to declare a new variable is done as follows:

   ```
   struct structure-name variable-name;
   ```

   or

   ```
   struct structure-name variable-name-list;
   ```

   where structure-name has been previously defined.

4. Values are given to a structure variable in the following manner:

   ```
   variable-name.member-name = expression;
   ```

   Recent UNIX compilers allow you to assign the values in one structure to another structure:

   ```
   variable-name = variable-name
   ```

   Older and non-UNIX compilers often require you to assign values within the structure member by member (a way around this limitation is to use pointers, that is, p = q, where p and q are pointers to structures).

5. You cannot normally pass a structure as an argument to a function on most compilers; you may pass a pointer to the structure to a function. Beginning with UNIX System V versions of c, structures were allowed as arguments (you can also return a structure as a result of a function); do not expect this construct to be portable between all compilers.

6. A special type of integer variable is allowed in a structure: variable-length bit fields. The number of bits is specified within the declaration as follows:

```
struct structure-name
{
        int name:bits;
               .
               .
               .
};
```

where name is the member to be assigned, and the number following the colon is the number of bits to assign.

An unnamed bit field specified with a width of 0 (zero) insures that the next field starts with a word boundary (any declaration line without a bit field automatically starts at the next word boundary).

When you use such bit field variables, bit members are packed into int type variables for convenience of storage by the c compiler (some recent versions of UNIX c pack into char, short, or long fields, as well). Bit-field members are referred to in the same manner as any other declared member.

7. Recursive use of structure definitions are allowed.

Defaults

See #3 above.

Example

Sample use:

```
struct YOUR
{
        char name[10];
        int age;
        double wages;
        int sex:1;      /* one bit assigned to sex */
        int :0;         /* align next on boundary */
        int race:2;     /* two bits assigned to race */
};
struct YOUR record;
record.name = name;
record.age = 30;
record.wages = 45.32;
record.sex = 1;
record.race = 3;
```

struct

Exceptions

Some compilers do not allow you to set one structure equal to another, pass structures as an argument, or return structures as results.

Returns

Not applicable.

typedef

Name

typedef

Format

```
typedef type name;
```

Purpose

The typedef keyword allows you to define your own synonyms for data storage classes. It is useful in reducing complicated type declarations, used repeatedly throughout a program, to a single, defining word.

Usage Rules

1. Typedef is a defining statement. Everything that appears between the word "typedef" and the name is defined as being associated with the name. In other words, if you have

    ```
    typedef int name;
    ```

    All later occurrences of "name" are then replaced with "int."

2. The name you use in a typedef statement should not conflict with variable or function names you assign.

3. Typedef is especially useful for creating a single data type in portable programs when the compilers you're using don't agree on data type definitions. For instance, one compiler has 8-bit chars, the other 16-bit chars, so you define a metachar type to be a consistent bit length on both:

    ```
    compiler 1: typedef short int metachar;
    compiler 2: typedef char metachar;
    ```

Defaults

None.

Example

Sample use:

```
typedef unsigned long int *point;
point p1, p2, p3;
```

Exceptions

None.

Returns

Not applicable.

union

Name

union

Format

```
union union-name {member-declaration-list};
union union-name {member-declaration-list}; variable-name;
union union-name {member-declaration-list}; variable-name =
value;
```

Purpose

A union is a single variable whose storage allocation is large enough so that any one of several different member variables may be present at any given time.

Usage Rules

1. The compiler reserves space only for the largest data type declared in a union. The compiler does not keep track of what data type currently resides in the union variable; this is the responsibility of the programmer. A "tag field" is often used to indicate the type of the current contents of the union:

```
struct
{
     int tag;
     union
     {
          .
          .
     };
};
```

2. Unions are defined in the same manner as structures (see struct, page 33). The usage rules for structures also apply to unions, including those of bit fields.

3. A semicolon must appear after the closing curly bracket (}) in a union definition.

Defaults

None.

Example

Sample use:

```
union AFLCIO
{
     char pres[4];
     float sec;
};
union AFLCIO striker;
```

union

```
striker.pres[0] = 't';
striker.pres[1] = 'e';
striker.pres[2] = 'h';
```

Exceptions

Some compilers do not implement unions.

Returns

Not applicable.

unsigned

Name

unsigned

Format

```
unsigned type name;
unsigned type name-list;
class unsigned type name;
class unsigned type name-list;
```

Purpose

The unsigned modifier tells the compiler to use the sign bit (usually the high-order bit) of the variable for values rather than negation.

Usage Rules

1. Values stored in an unsigned variable must be zero or greater (positive in value). The following is generally true of most compilers:

   unsigned char = 0 to 255
   unsigned int =   0 to 65,635
   unsigned long = 0 to 4,294,967,295

2. Unsigned variables are often used for pointers, since pointers are never negative values.

Defaults

If no variable type is specified, a type of int is assumed.

Example

Sample use:

```
unsigned int aquarius;
aquarius = pisces = 3;
```

Exceptions

Remember some compilers have different bit counts for int and long type variables, meaning a different range of possible numbers than those stated in rule #1, above. Also, most compilers only allow unsigned int types; unsigned char and unsigned long are only implemented on some compilers.

Returns

Not applicable.

3

Defining Functions

Defining and Formatting Functions

A function is a set of c statements grouped together by the programmer because they define one task (or group of tasks) to be done, or otherwise seem to go together as a unit. A valid c program must contain at least one function, named main (see below). Other common functions are often predefined for the programmer by the compiler creator (see Sections 7 through 10).

When a particular function (or task, if you will) has not been predefined, the c programmer must create a new function. The required format of a function definition is as follows:

```
name(arguments)
argument declarations;
{
    other declarations;
    statements;
}
```

This is the bare minimum format for a function. The "name" is the name you have chosen for the function. Naming conventions for functions generally follow those of variables:

- The function name must start with a letter or underscore, and should be in lowercase letters only for maximum portability.
- Digits are permitted, but only after the initial letter.
- Only the first 6 characters (digits or letters) should be considered significant, although this number varies among compilers.
- Keywords cannot be used (see list on page 3).

The function name is followed by its argument list, contained in parentheses immediately following the name. The argument list contains the variables used to pass information to the function, when necessary. An argument list is not necessary if no information is being passed to the function, but the parentheses must remain. The line that contains the function name and argument list is NOT terminated by a semicolon when defining a function. Functions must have the parentheses, even if no arguments are passed to it. Arguments are enclosed in the parentheses; no space normally follows the function name (some compilers allow spaces, while others do not).

Next come the argument declarations (the assignment of data types). Any variable which appears in the argument list but is not declared is considered to default to type int. Argument declarations are terminated by semicolons, just as within the main c program code.

An opening brace is ({) used to declare the start of the actual function proper. An ending brace (}) declares the end of the function definition. Within the braces may come internal argument declarations (arguments internal to the function), and valid c statements, including calls to functions.

A function definition may be much more complicated, as well. Here is the format of a function with all the function defining options used.

```
type name(arguments)
argument declarations;
{
```

```
        internal declarations;
        statements;
        return value;
}
```

A data "type" for the function must be declared if the function is to pass information of a type other than int back to the c statements that called it. Whenever a function is of a type other than int, you must also declare the called function's type in the calling function. The data type declared (preceding the function name) should match the data type of the "value" in the return statement within the function. Otherwise, the compiler will convert the value to the declared type, with possibly unwanted results.

Functions are like variables, in that they can have a value and be put into a statement anywhere a variable can (to the right of the equal sign). A popular example of this is

```
response = getchar();
(where getchar() is a function.)
```

Functions may be defined in any order. Use a system of ordering that helps you find them quickly.

You may not define a function within a function, but functions may call themselves directly or indirectly (through other functions). Recursion is allowed.

The preferred format is:

```
/*      This function returns the value of
 *      a number times itself (squared).
 */
int square(number)
int number;
{
        int result;

        result = number * number;
        return result;
        /* note that the above statement could have
         * been:  return number * number;
         */
}
```

Alternate format:

```
/*      This function returns the value of
 *      a number times itself (squared).
 */
int
square(number)
        int number;
        {
        int result;

        result = number * number;
        return result;
        }
```

Variable Usage in Functions

Variable usage must be carefully considered when programming in c. Since the manner in which functions are defined plays a primary role in determining the "scope" of a variable (where it is or isn't active), it seems proper to address the problem of variable usage at length here.

Variables should be defined at the start of the function. This is especially true for automatic variables, whose space is allocated only when they are active within the function. It is too easy to later add code and not have a variable defined if you scatter variable declarations throughout the function..

c uses a "modern" approach to programming languages in that arguments are passed to a function by value, as do Algol, Pascal, and PL/I. This means the function has to create a copy of the argument (the function can change this copy at will). Because of this anomaly, the value in the "calling" portion of the program is not actually changed by the function. If the function returns a value back to the calling portion of the program, this value may be used to change the value of the original argument, but during the execution of the function the value does not change.

An exception to the above rule occurs when the argument passed to a function is a pointer. The pointer value cannot be directly changed by the function, but the contents of the variable pointed to *can* be. Thus, if you wish to circumvent the argument-passed-by-value aspect of c, you pass the pointer as an argument to the variable you want to directly manipulate, instead using the variable itself as the argument.

One point that catches many c novices by surprise is that the names of arrays, structures, and strings are actually pointers to the actual data. Therefore, arrays, structures, and strings passed as arguments to a function are passed as pointers, allowing direct manipulation of the data by the function.

An example that shows the above rules might be:

```
main()
{
        int number;
        char array[10];
        function(number, array);
}

void function(number, array);
char array[];
{
        number = 3;       /* doesn't change number in main */
        array[0] = 'a';      /* DOES change array in main */
}
```

Values can be passed between functions as arguments, returns, or external variables. The only other way to manipulate information between functions is by using pointers, as described above, to directly manipulate information. You should note arguments are normally passed to a function as values only except for externally declared variables. The actual variables tend to be private to a function.

main

Name

main

Format

```
main()
main(arguments)*
```
*normally argc, argv

main

return

Purpose

The main function is the primary function of a c program and marks the beginning of executable c statements.

Usage Rules

1. The main function provides the base of a c program. All other executable statements reside in other functions, which are called directly or indirectly from within the main function. The main function is where the program execution begins.

2. The main function is usually passed two pieces of information, called argc and argv. argc contains the number of arguments typed, including the filename, when the program was invoked. argv is an array of pointers to the arguments. argv[0] points to the actual program (file name) in which main is contained (what was typed at the operating system level to start the program). The arguments are stored as strings (terminated with \0).

Defaults

None.

Example

Sample use:

```
main(argc,argv)
int argc;
char **argv;
{
      int i;
      for (i = 0; i < argc; i++)
      printf("%s, ",argv[i]);
}
```

Exceptions

None.

Returns

Not applicable.

return

Name

return

Format

```
return;
return expression;
```

Purpose

The return statement is used to terminate the execution of the current function, return control to the calling function, and, if an expression is present, to pass the resulting value to the calling function.

Usage Rules

1. If no argument follows the return statement, no value is passed to the calling function. If an argument (expression) follows the return statement, the value of that expression is returned to the calling function.

2. The expression must reduce to a value of the same data type as the function declared. If the function was not explicitly given a data type, the value must be of type int.

3. If the expression following return is complicated, some programmers use parentheses to distinguish the expression from return; this is not necessary.

Defaults

Use of a function name on the righthand side of an assignment statement will always yield a value even if the function does not return one. "Unplanned" returned values from functions are nonsensical and may cause your program to behave erratically.

Example

Sample use:

```
int isnumber(c)
char c;
{
        if ( '0' <= c && c <= '9' )
            return TRUE;
    else
            return FALSE;
}
```

Exceptions

None.

Returns

The value of the expression that immediately follows the word "return."

4

Operators and Symbols

The Nomenclature of Operators

An operator is a symbol that represents an operation (function) to be performed with one or more pieces of information, called operands.

Kernighan and Ritchie divide operators into several classes, most notably

- primary-expression
- unary
- binary
- assignment

While this nomenclature is useful in remembering the priority of the operators, it mixes the notions of purpose and description. The term "primary-expression operators," for instance, tells what these operators do: they serve to define which of the operands (arguments, if you will) have primacy over the others. The term "unary operator," however, describes the number of operands the operator works on.

With the exception of the Precedence of Operators section immediately following, this book will name operators according to their function, as opposed to the traditional Kernighan and Ritchie manner. Not only does it make clearer the purpose the operators serve, it also serves to more closely divide the operators according to function, as opposed to priority.

Precedence (Priority) of Operators

The following priorities are used in determining which portion of an expression or statement is evaluated first. Each line down on the page indicates a lower priority than the one above it. Items on the same priority level are considered to have equal priority, and are calculated in the direction indicated by the arrows (right-to-left, left-to-right). This is called "grouping." The numbers in parentheses are the priority level; higher numbers mean higher priority.

Primary-expression operators:

( ) [ ] . ->   ----> (15) highest priority

Unary operators:

* & - ! ~ ++ -- sizeof (type)   <---- (14)

Binary operators:

* / %	----> (13)
+ -	----> (12)
>> <<	----> (11)
< > <= >=	----> (10)
== !=	----> (9)
&	----> (8)

```
  ^                          ----> ( 7)
  |                          ----> ( 6)
  &&                         ----> ( 5)
  | |                        ----> ( 4)
  ?:                         <---- ( 3)
```

Assignment operators:

```
  = += -= *= /= %=           <---- (2)
  >> =< <= &= ^= |=
```

Sequence operator:

```
  ,(comma)                   ----> (1) lowest priority
```

A simple example that shows why knowing priority of operators is necessary might be something like this:

```
  a = b + c / d;
```

In the above example, the result stored in variable a will be different depending upon whether the division or the addition is done first. Since
division (/) has a higher priority than addition (+), variable c is first divided
by variable d, then the result is added to the value in variable b.

Type Conversion of Operators

During the evaluation of an expression containing operators, it is sometimes necessary to convert data from one type to another (you may sometimes intermix data types in expressions). The following rules are used to
determine the conversion of data types:

1. In arithmetic operations, the highest ranking operand determines the
result and other operands are converted to that type.
    In assignment operations, the value placed in the right operand of
the assignment is first converted to the type of the operand on the left.
Truncation or rounding may occur, as in the arithmetic operations.

rank	type	effect on data
1	double	rounded to float truncated to long, int, char
2	float	padded with zeroes to double truncated to long, int, char
3	long	truncated to int, char
4	int	padded with sign bits (unless declared as unsigned, then padded with zero bits) to long truncated to char
5	char	padded with sign bits (unless declared as unsigned, then padded with zero bits) to int

2. Char data types are always converted to type int for arithmetic calculations or if passed in arguments to functions.

3. Numbers of type float are promoted to the type of double before arithmetic is performed, then rounded to float or truncated to int type results, if necessary.

4. Numbers of type float are promoted to the type of double before being passed as arguments to functions.

5. You may "cast" (force) a conversion of an expression to a particular data type by using the following format:

```
(type) expression
```

as in

```
result = (int) (pi * radius);
```

where result, pi, and radius are all float or double numbers. This forces the product of "pi" times "radius" to be first converted to an integer (causing truncation, which is presumed desirable) and then converted from integer back to the type of "result."

Address Operators

*

Operator

* (indirection operator)

Function

The *, when used as a prefix to an integer variable name, yields the value at the address contained by the variable. The bit pattern of the fetched value is assumed to be of the declared data type of the variable, although there is no assurance that this is the correct bit pattern.

Example

```
int *variable, result;
variable = (int *) 0x100;
result = *variable;
```

Yields the integer value at the address 100 hex.

Restrictions

The variable * is used with must be a pointer (exception: reference to an absolute memory location can be performed, as in *(0x10) = 0;, which sets location 10 hex to a value of 0). There should be no space between the operand and the operator.

Order

The expression groups from right to left.

Precedence

Level 14 of 15.

Special Note

You might occasionally see something like this:

```
char **name[ ]
```

This is a variable that is a pointer to a pointer to an array of char, where

```
char *name[ ];
```

is a pointer to an array of chars, and

```
char name[ ];
```

is an array of chars.

The use of two consecutive indirection operators (**) does not change the meaning, it simply means there are two operators, the second of which operates on the operand, the first of which operates on the second * operand:

```
*    *    name
     └────┬────┘
```

* is operator, name is operand

```
└────────┬────────┘
```

* is operator, *name is operand

&

Operator

& (address operator)

Function

The &, when used as a prefix to a variable name, yields the address of the variable.

Example

```
int variable, *result;
result = &variable;
```

Yields the address of "variable."

Restrictions

The variable & is used with must be a reference to a value. It is illegal to take the address of an expression. For example

```
result = &(value + 1);    /* illegal construct */
```

No space should appear between the operator and the operand.

Order

The expression groups from right to left.

Precedence

Level 14 of 15.

[ ]

Operator

[ ] (array operator)

Function

The square brackets indicate the presence of an array. The value in the brackets is used to offset the address of the array's beginning in order to determine the amount of memory needed for storage (when used in a variable declaration), or to determine the proper address for the specified element (when used in an assignment statement).

Example

```
int number [9], result;
result = number[3];
```

The value of result is determined by what is stored in the fourth memory location of the array number (beginning plus 3).

Restrictions

Either the variable or the array reference must refer to an address. Empty brackets (nothing between them) are legal in only three instances:

1. Passing a declared array's initial address to a declaration in a function:

```
function (args)
int args[ ]; /* address passed! */
```

2. When an array is initialized and the number of elements can be determined by context:

```
int array [ ] = {1,2,3};
```

3. When declared externally, and the definition appears elsewhere:

```
extern int array[ ];
```

No space should appear between the operand and the operator.

Order

The expression groups from left to right.

Precedence

Level 15 of 15 (highest level).

Operator

. (structure address operator)

Function

The . operator, when used to separate two variables, yields the value of the second variable's field within the structure of the first variable.

Example

```
result = one.two;
```

The result is the value of the field "two" within structure "one."

NOTE: the example is equivalent to

```
result = (&one)->two;
```

Restrictions

The variable following the . operator must be a structure field; the variable preceding . the operator must be a structure. The field specified must be part of the specified structure, or unexpected results will occur. No space should appear between the operator and the operands.

Order

The expression groups from left to right.

Precedence

Level 15 of 15 (highest priority).

->

Operator

-> (structure pointer operator)

Function

The -> (minus sign followed by the greater than sign) operator is similar to the . operator, but yields the value of the second variable's field found in the structure beginning at the address of the first variable. The structure pointer operator -> is normally used (instead of using the structure address operator .) when the value of the pointer (first operand) is calculated by some previous statement(s) in the program or passed as an argument.

Example

```
result = ptr->one;
```

result becomes the value of the "one" field within the structure that begins at the address referred to by "ptr."

NOTE: the example is the same as

```
result = (*ptr).one;
```

Exceptions

The variable preceding the -> operator must be a pointer to a structure; the variable following the operator must be a structure field. The structure pointed to should contain the structure field referenced, or unpredictable results may result. No space should appear between the operator and the operands.

Order

Evaluation of the expression is done from left to right.

Precedence

Level 15 of 15 (highest priority).

Arithmetic Operators

+

Operator

+ (addition operator)

Function

Yields the sum of the two operands.

Example

```
int a = 4;
int b = 2;
int result;
result = a + b;
```

result is the sum of variable a's value added to variable b's value (6).

Restrictions

If one operand is a pointer, the other must be an integer or char variable (see discussion on incrementation of pointers, page 16). NOTE: this operation may create an overflow in the variable, making the results erroneous.

Order

The expression groups from left to right.

Precedence

Level 12 of 15.

Operator

- (subtraction, or difference, operator)

Function

The - operator, when used between two operands, yields the difference between the first and second operands.

Example

```
/* difference example */
int a = 4;
int b = 2;
int result;
result = a - b;
```

result becomes the value of variable a less the value of variable b (2).

NOTE: it is easy to confuse the binary subtraction operator and the unary negation operator. The former should always be followed by a space, the latter should never be followed by a space. Parentheses around the negation emphasize it.

Restrictions

When the - operator is used to calculate the difference between operands where either operand is a pointer, the second operand must be either: a) an integer or char type variable, or b) a pointer of the same data type (see discussion of pointer incrementation on page 16).

Order

The expression groups from left to right.

Precedence

Level 12 of 15.

-

Operator

- (negation operator)

Function

The - operator, when used with a single operand, yields the arithmetic negation of the operand.

Example

```
/* negation example */
int a = 4;
int result;
result = (-a);
```

result is the arithmetic negation of the value of the variable (-4).

NOTE: it is easy to confuse the binary subtraction operator and the unary negation operator. The former should always be followed by a space, the latter should never be followed by a space. Parentheses around the negation emphasize it.

Restrictions

When the - operator is used to imply arithmetic negation, neither operand may be a pointer. When the - operator is used as a negation operator, no space should appear between the operator and the operand. Note that the - operator can produce an overflow under some circumstances, causing erroneous results.

Order

The expression groups from right to left.

Precedence

Level 14 of 15.

++

Operator

++ (increment operator)

Function

The ++ operator increments the referenced operand.

Example

```
int result, a = 4;
result = ++a;
```

result is the value of the variable incremented by one (5). Note the value of variable a is also changed!

Restrictions

The placement of the ++ operator in relationship to the operand tells the compiler whether to perform the incrementation before or after using the referenced operand.

++operand   Increment BEFORE using operand in expression.
operand++   Increment AFTER using operand in expression.

An example:

```
int a, b;
int c = 1;
c++;        /* c = 2 after this statement */
++c;        /* c = 3 now                   */
a = ++c;    /* a = 4, c = 4                */
b = c++;    /* b = 4, c = 5                */
```

The operand in question must be a numeric value or a pointer. No space should appear between the operand and the operator. Incrementation may create a variable overflow.

NOTE: when pointers are incremented, they are not incremented by a value of 1, but are incremented to point to the next object (its address).

Order

The expression groups from right to left.

Precedence

Level 14 of 15.

Operator

-- (decrement operator)

Function

The -- operator decrements the referenced operand.

Example

```
int result, a = 4;
result = a--;
```

result is the value of the variable. The variable is decremented by one (result = 4, a = 3).

Restrictions

The placement of the -- operator in relationship to the operand tells the compiler whether to perform the decrementation before or after using the referenced operand.

--operand   Decrement BEFORE using operand in expression.
operand--   Decrement AFTER using operand in expression.

An example:

```
int a, b;
int c = 10;
c--;        /* c = 9 after  this  statement */
--c;        /* c = 8 now                     */
a = --c;    /* a = 7, c = 7                   */
b = c--;    /* b = 7, c = 6                   */
```

The operand in question must be a numeric value or a pointer. No space should appear between the operand and the operator. Decrementation may create a variable overflow.

NOTE: when pointers are decremented, they are not decremented by a value of 1, but are decremented to point to the previous object (its address).

Order

The expression groups from right to left.

Precedence

Level 14 of 15.

*

Operator

* (multiplication operator)

Function

Yields the product of the two operands.

Example

```
int a = 4, b = 2;
long result;
result = (long) a * b;
```

result is the product of the value of the variable and the value of variable b (8).

Restrictions

The operands cannot be pointers. Unlike some programming languages, multiplying two variables of the same type does not automatically produce a result of double precision. Unless you cast at least one operand (see the cast operator, page 94), the result may overflow its assigned storage.

Order

The expression groups from left to right.

Precedence

Level 13 of 15.

/

Operator

/ (division operator)

Function

The / operator yields the quotient of the first operand divided by the second. The remainder is not available or used for int type variables.

Example

```
int a = 6, b = 2;
int result;
result = a / b;
```

Result is the quotient of the division of variable a's value by variable b's value (quotient is the whole, not fractional, portion of the division—3).

Exceptions

The operands many not be pointers. Division by zero gives compiler dependent results (both overflow and underflow conditions are possible, depending upon the implementation).

Order

The expression groups from left to right.

Precedence

Level 13 of 15.

%

Operator

% (modulus operator)

Function

The % operator yields the remainder (modulus) of the division of the first operand by the second. The quotient is not used.

Example

```
int a = 5;
int b = 2;
int result;
result = a % b;
```

result is the remainder of the division of the value of variable a divided by the value of the variable b (1).

Restrictions

The operands must not be of the type double or float, and must not be pointers.

Order

The expression groups from left to right.

Precedence

Level 13 of 15.

Assignment Operators

=

Operator

= (assignment operator)

Function

The operand preceding the = operator takes on the value of the operand following the operator.

NOTE: the equal sign (assignment operator) is not the same as two equal signs (= =, the equivalence operator). Mixing these two operators up is a common problem for newcomers to c.

Example

```
int a = 4;
int result;
result = a;
```

result takes on the value of the a variable (4).

Restrictions

The operands may be of any type, except arrays. For reasons of program style, one space should appear on either side of the operator. The data type of the second operand will be converted to the type of the first operand. Assignment operators used with structures may not be supported by all compilers.

Order

The expression groups from right to left.

Precedence

Level 2 of 15.

+=

Operator

+= (addition assignment operator)

Function

The operand preceding the += operator takes on the value resulting from the sum of it and the operand following the operator.

x += y is equivalent to x = (x) + (y)

Example

```
int a = 4;
int b = 2;
b += a;
```

b takes of the value of b plus a (6).

Restrictions

The operands may be of any type other than an array or structure. Only the first operator (lefthand side of the assignment) can be a pointer. For example:

```
int *p, *q;
p += q;        /* WRONG! error occurs */
```

For reasons of program style, one space should appear on either side of the operator. A data overflow is possible with this operator.

Order

The expression groups from right to left.

Precedence

Level 2 of 15.

- =

Operator

-= (subtraction assignment operator)

Function

The operand preceding the -= operator takes on the value obtained by subtracting the second operand from it.

x -= y is equivalent to x = (x) - (y)

Example

```
int a = 4;
int b = 2;
b -= a;
```

b takes of the value of b minus the value of a (2).

Restrictions

The operands may be of any type other than an array or structure. Only the first operator (lefthand side of the assignment) can be a pointer. For example:

```
int *p, *q;
p -= q;          /* WRONG! error occurs */
```

For reasons of program style, one space should appear on either side of the operator. A data overflow is possible with this operator.

Order

The expression groups from right to left.

Precedence

Level 2 of 15.

✳ =

Operator

✳= (multiplication assignment operator)

Function

The operand preceding the ✳= operator takes on the value resulting from the product of the two operands.

x ✳= y is equivalent to x = (x) ✳ (y)

Example

```
int a = 4;
int b = 2;
b *= a;
```

b takes of the value of b times the value of a (8).

Restrictions

The operands may be of any type other than a pointer, array, or structure. For reasons of program style, one space should appear on either side of the operator. A data overflow is possible with this operator.

Order

The expression groups from right to left.

Precedence

Level 2 of 15.

/=

Operator

/= (division assignment operator)

Function

The operand preceding the /= operator takes on the quotient resulting from division of the second operand by the first.

x /= y is equivalent to x = (x) / (y)

Example

```
int a = 4;
int b = 2;
b /= a;
```

b takes of the quotient of b divided by the value of a (2).

Restrictions

The operands may be of any type other than a pointer, an array, or structure. For reasons of program style, one space should appear on either side of the operator. A data overflow is possible with this operator.

Order

The expression groups from right to left.

Precedence

Level 2 of 15.

%=

Operator

% = (modulus assignment operator)

Function

The operand preceding the % = operator takes on the remainder resulting from division of the second operator by the first.

x % = y is equivalent to x = (x) % (y)

Example

```
int a = 4;
int b = 2;
b %= a;
```

b takes of the remainder of b divided by the value of a (0).

Restrictions

The operands may be of any type other than a pointer, float, array, or structure. For reasons of program style, one space should appear on either side of the operator.

Order

The expression groups from right to left.

Precedence

Level 2 of 15.

>>=

Operator

>>= (shift right assignment operator)

Function

The first operand is shifted right the number of bits indicated by the second operand.

x >>= y is equivalent to x = (x) >> (y)

Example

```
int a = 4;
int result = 2;
result >>= a;
```

result is the value of result shifted right the number of bits in the value of a.

Restrictions

The operands may be of any integer or char type other than a pointer, array, or structure. For reasons of program style, one space should appear on either side of the operator. The righthand side (second operand) must be of an integral type. The right shift may be performed logically (zeroes added to fill result) or arithmetic (the sign bit is repeated), and this action is usually dependent upon the data type of the first operand (signed operands get arithmetic right shifts while unsigned operands get logically right shifts).

It is normal practice to parenthesize this operation when it is combined with other relational operators.

```
x = ( ( y >>= z ) <<= a );
```

This operation may cause variable overflow.

You should not use the >>= operator with signed numbers; doing so loses the sign on some compilers, discouraging program portability. If you must use signed variables, cast (force) the type to be unsigned, as in

```
(unsigned)~z >>= a
```

The result is undefined if the right operand is negative, or if the value of the right operand is greater than or equal to the length of the left operand.

Order

The expression groups from right to left.

Precedence

Level 2 of 15.

<<=

Operator

<<= (shift left assignment operator)

Function

<<= operand yields the result of the first operand shifted left by the number of bits indicated by the second operand.

x <<= y is equivalent to x = (x) << (y)

Example

```
int a = 4;
int result = 2;
result <<= a;
```

result is the value of result shifted left by the number of bits in the value of a.

Restrictions

The operands may be of any integer or char data type other than a pointer, array, or structure. For reasons of program style, one space should appear on either side of the operator. The righthand side (second operand) must be of an integral type.

This operator may create variable overflow. The left shift operator is performed logically, not arithmetically (in other words, zeroes fill the missing bits).

It is normal practice to parenthesize this operation when it is combined with other relational operators.

```
x = ( ( y == z ) <<= a );
```

This operation may cause variable overflow.

The result is undefined if the right operand is negative, or the value of the right operand is greater than or equal to the length of the left operand.

Order

The expression groups from right to left.

Precedence

Level 2 of 15.

&=

Operator

&= (bitwise AND assignment operator)

Function

The &= operand yields the result of the first operand ANDed bit by bit with the second operand.

x &= y is equivalent to x = (x) & (y)

Example

```
int a = 4;
int result = 2;
result &= a;
```

result is the value of result ANDed bit by bit with the value of a (non-zero).

Restrictions

The operands may be of any type other than a pointer, array, or structure. For reasons of program style, one space should appear on either side of the operator. Normally, both sides of the assignment (both operands) are integral.

Order

The expression groups from right to left.

Precedence

Level 2 of 15.

|=

Operator

|= (bitwise inclusive OR assignment operator)

Function

The |= operator yields the result of the first operand ORed bit by bit with the second operand.

x |= y is equivalent to x = (x)|(y)

Example

```
int a = 4;
int result = 2;
result | = a;
```

result is the value of result inclusive ORed bit by bit with the value of a (non-zero).

Restrictions

The operands may be of any type other than a pointer, array, or structure. For reasons of program style, one space should appear on either side of the operator. Normally, both sides of the assignment (both operands) are integral.

Order

The expression groups from right to left.

Precedence

Level 2 of 15.

^=

Operator

^= (bitwise exclusive OR assignment operator)

Function

The ^= operand yields the result of the first operand exclusive ORed bit by bit with the second operand.

x ^= y is equivalent to x = (x) ^ (y)

Example

```
int a = 4;
int result = 2;
result = a;
```

result is the value of result exclusive ORed with the value of a (zero).

Restrictions

The operands may be of any type other than a pointer, array, or structure. For reasons of program style, one space should appear on either side of the operator. Normally, both sides of the assignment (both operands) are integral.

Order

The expression groups from right to left.

Precedence

Level 2 of 15.

Bitwise Operators

&

Operator

& (bitwise AND operator)

Function

The & function performs the bitwise AND of the two operands.

Operand1		Operand2		Result
1	&	1	=	1
1	&	0	=	0
0	&	1	=	0
0	&	0	=	0

where 1 = true and 0 = false.

Example

```
int a = 3;
int b = 4;
int result;
result = a & b.
```

result is the bitwise ANDing of the values of a and b.

Restrictions

The operands must be of integer or char data types. It is normal practice to parenthesize this operation when it is combined with other relational operators.

```
x = ( ( y >> z ) & a ) ;
```

Order

The expression groups from left to right.

Precedence

Level 8 of 15.

Operator

| (bitwise inclusive OR operator)

Function

The operator performs the bitwise inclusive ORing of the two operands.

Operand1	Operand2		Result
1	1	=	0
1	0	=	1
0	1	=	1
0	0	=	0

Example

```
int a = 5;
int b = 2;
int result;
result = a|b;
```

result is the bitwise ORing of a and b.

Restrictions

The operands must be of integer or char data types. It is normal practice to parenthesize this operation when it is combined with other relational operators.

```
x = (( y >> z )|a );
```

Order

The expression groups from left to right.

Precedence

Level 6 of 15.

Operator

^ (bitwise exclusive OR operator)

Function

The ^ operator performs the bitwise exclusive ORing of the two operands.

Operand1		Operand2		Result
1	^	1	=	0
1	^	0	=	1
0	^	1	=	1
0	^	0	=	0

Example

```
int a = 9;
int b = 4;
int result;
result = a ^ b
```

result is the bitwise exclusive ORing of the values of a and b.

Restrictions

The operands must be of integer or char data types. It is normal practice to parenthesize this operation when it is combined with other relational operators.

```
x = ( ( y >> z ) ^ a );
```

Order

The expression groups from left to right.

Precedence

Level 7 of 15.

Operator

~ (one's complement operator)

Function

The operator yields the bitwise one's complement of its single operand (ones become zeroes, zeroes become ones).

Example

```
int a = 5;
int result;
result = (~a)
```

result is the one's complement of the value of a.

Restrictions

The operands must be of integer or char data types. No space should appear between the operand and the operator. It is normal practice to parenthesize this operation when it is combined with other relational operators.

```
x = ( ( y >> z ) (~a) );
```

Order

The expression groups from left to right.

Precedence

Level 14 of 15.

<<

Operator

<< (shift left operator)

Function

The << operator yields the first operand shifted left the number of bits specified by the second operand. Zeroes (0) are shifted into the low-order bits that have been displaced.

Example

```
int a = 6;
int b = 1;
int result;
result = a << b;
```

result is the value of variable a shifted left the number of bits equal to the value of variable b.

Restrictions

The operands must be of integer or char data types. It is normal practice to parenthesize this operation when it is combined with other relational operators.

```
x = ( ( y >> z ) << a );
```

This operation may cause variable overflow.

The result is undefined if the right operand is negative, or the value of the right operand is greater than or equal to the length of the left operand.

Order

The expression groups from left to right.

Precedence

Level 11 of 15.

Operator

>> (shift right operator)

Function

The >> operator yields the first operand shifted right the number of bits specified by the second operand. Zeroes (0) are shifted into the high-order bits if the first operand is an unsigned number, while the sign bit is duplicated if the first operand is signed.

Example

```
int a = 65;
int b = 5;
int result;
result = a >> b;
```

result is the value of variable a shifted right the number of bits specified by the value of variable b.

Restrictions

The operands must be of integer or char data types. It is normal practice to parenthesize this operation when it is combined with other relational operators.

```
x = (( y >> z ) << a );
```

This operation may cause variable overflow.

You should not use the >> operator with signed numbers; doing so loses the sign on some compilers, discouraging program portability. If you must use signed variables, cast (force) the type to be unsigned, as in

```
(unsigned)-z >> a
```

The result is undefined if the right operand is negative, if the value of the right operand is greater than or equal to the length of the left operand.

Order

The expression groups from left to right.

Precedence

Level 11 of 15.

Logical Operators

&&

Operator

&& (logical AND operator)

Function

The && operator yields the logical ANDing of the two operands.

Operand1	Operand2	Result
non-zero	non-zero	non-zero
non-zero	zero	zero
zero	non-zero	zero
zero	zero	zero

Example

```
double a = 456;
double b = 123;
int result;
result = a && b;
```

result is the logical ANDing of the values of the two operands, a and b (non-zero).

Restrictions

The result is an integer; the operands may be numbers or pointers.

The operation is considered completed the moment the result is known (if the first operand is zero, it makes no difference what the second is!). The second operand may not be evaluated.

Order

The left operand is guaranteed to be calculated first.

Precedence

Level 5 of 15.

||

Operator

|| (logical inclusive OR operator)

Function

The || function yields the logical inclusive OR of the two operands.

Operand1	Operand2	Result
non-zero	non-zero	non-zero
non-zero	zero	non-zero
zero	non-zero	non-zero
zero	zero	zero

Example

```
if ( a < b || b < c)
printf("a is less than b\n and/or b is less than c");
```

Restrictions

The result is an integer; the operands must be of integer or char data types.
   The operation is considered completed the moment the result is known (if the first operand is non-zero, the result must be non-zero!). The second operand may not be evaluted.

Order

The left operand is guaranteed to be calculated first.

Precedence

Level 4 of 15.

!

Operator

! (logical negation operator)

Function

The ! operator yields the logical negation of the single operand that follows it (non-zero if the operand is equal to zero, 0 if the operand is not zero).

Example

```
int a = 1;
int result;
result = !a;
```

result is the logical negation of the value of a (zero).

Restrictions

The result is an integer; the operands may be numbers or pointers. No space should appear between the operand and the operator.

Order

The expression groups from right to left.

Precedence

Level 14 of 15.

Comparative Operators

<

Operator

< (less than operator)

Function

The < operand yields non-zero if the first operand is less than the second operand; zero (0) otherwise.

Example

```
if (a<b)
printf('a was less than b');
```

Restrictions

Result is of type integer; operands may be a number, char, or pointer. Use the same type (number or pointer) for both operands to get consistent results. Chars and numbers may be compared; chars convert to ints as in arithmetic (see page 49).

Order

The expression groups from left to right.

Precedence

Level 10 of 15.

>

Operator

> (greater than operator)

Function

The > operand yields non-zero if the first operand is greater than the second operand; zero (0) otherwise.

Example

```
if (a>b)
    printf("a was greater than b");
```

Restrictions

Result is of type integer; operands may be a number, char, or pointer. Use same type (number or pointer) for both operands to ensure consistent results. Chars and numbers may be compared; chars convert to ints as in arithmetic (see page 49).

Order

The expression groups from left to right.

Precedence

Level 10 of 15.

<=

Operator

< = (less than or equal to operator)

Function

The < = operator yields non-zero if the first operand is less than or equal to the second; zero (0) otherwise.

Example

```
if (a <= b)
      printf("a is not greater than b");
```

Restrictions

Result is of type integer; the operands may be numbers, chars, or pointers. Use the same type (number or pointer) for both operands in order to ensure consistent results. Chars and numbers may be compared; chars convert to ints as in arithmetic (see page 49).

Order

The expression groups from left to right.

Precedence

Level 10 of 15.

>=

Operator

>= (greater than or equal to operator)

Function

The >= operator yields non-zero if the first operand is greater than or equal to the second; zero (0) otherwise.

Example

```
if (a >= b)
    printf("a is not less than b");
```

Restrictions

Result is of type integer; operands may be numbers, chars, or pointers. Use same type (number or pointer) for both operands to ensure consistent results. Chars and numbers may be compared; chars convert to ints as in arithmetic (see page 49).

Order

The expression groups from left to right.

Precedence

Level 10 of 15.

Operator

== (equality operator)

Function

The == operator yields non-zero if the first and second operands are logically equivalent; zero if not. NOTE: A common error is to accidentally put = (the assignment operator) in place of == (the equivalence operator). The compiler allows this substitution, but the results will not be what you expect. An example:

```
int a, b;
a = 1;
b = 0;
printf("%d %d %d", a, b, a==b);
printf("%d %d %d", a, b, a=b);
```

The example results in the following output:

```
1 0 0
0 0 0
```

Example

```
if (a == b)
    printf("a and b are logically equivalent");
```

Restrictions

The result is of type integer; the operands may be chars, numbers, or pointers. Use the same type (number or pointer) for both operands to ensure consistent results. Chars and numbers may be compared; chars convert to ints as in arithmetic (see page 49). Structures may not be compared.

Order

The expression groups from left to right.

Precedence

Level 9 of 15.

!=

Operator

!= (inequality operator)

Function

The != operator yields non-zero if the first and second operands are NOT logically equivalent; zero if they are.

Example

```
if (a != b)
    printf("a and b aren't logically the same");
```

Restrictions

The result is of type integer; the operands may be chars, numbers, or pointers. Use the same type (number or pointer) for both operands to ensure consistent results. Chars and numbers may be compared; chars convert to ints as in arithmetic (see page 49).

Order

The expression groups from left to right.

Precedence

Level 9 of 15.

?:

Operator

? : (conditional expression operator)

Function

The ? : operator yields the evaluation of the second operand if the first is non-zero; it yields the evaluation of the third operand otherwise.

Example

```
int x = 1;
char y = 'Y';
char z = 'N';
printf("%c\n",x?y:z);
```

Restrictions

None.

Order

The leftmost operand is guaranteed to be calculated first, before the second and third. Evaluation within the second or third operand is from right to left. Only one of the second and third operands is evaluated.

Precedence

Level 3 of 15.

!=

?:

Sequence Operator

,

Operator

, (sequence operator)

Function

The operand preceding the sequence (comma) operator is evaluated before the operand that follows.

Example

```
for(i = 1, j = 2; i == 2, j == 3; i++, j++)
    ;
```

Restrictions

None.

Order

The lefthand operand is guaranteed to be evaluated first; the righthand operand determines the logical value of the expression.

```
int i = 1;
int j = 0;
if (i == j, i == i)
        printf("case 1\n");
else
        printf("case 2\n");
```

yields the result of

```
case 1
```

Precedence

Level 1 of 15 (lowest priority).

Type Operators

sizeof

Operator

sizeof

Function

The sizeof operator yields the memory size of the operand in bytes.

Example

```
printf("%d\n",sizeof(a));
printf("%d\n",sizeof(char));
```

Restrictions

The operand may be any expression, including a data type specifier as in the second example above. A space should not follow the operator prior to the parentheses.

Order

The expression groups from right to left.

Precedence

Level 14 of 15.

(type) (casting operator)

Name

(type) (casting operator)

Function

The (type) operator yields (casts) the operand returned as the type speci-fied, regardless of the original type declaration of the variable(s) in the operand.

Example

```
int integer, number;
char character;
character = (char) integer;
number = (int) character;
```

Restrictions

The type must be enclosed in parentheses and be a storage type, like char, int, float, *int, *float, and so on (not a storage class).

Order

The expression groups from right to left.

Precedence

Level 14 of 15.

Symbolic Representations

Numbering Systems

All numbers are assumed to be decimal by the compiler unless one of the following special symbols appear:

0   The zero (0) prefix indicates the number that follows is in the octal base (base 8). Allowable characters following the 0 are 0 through 7, inclusive.

0x   The 0x prefix indicates the number that follows is in the hexadecimal base (base 16). Allowable characters following the 0x are 0 through 9, 'a' through 'f', and 'A' through 'F' inclusive.

L or l   The L or l (where l is the lowercase letter "L") suffix indicates that the number that precedes it is to be considered to be of type long.

Appendix D is a full listing of the ASCII code in the decimal, binary, octal, and hexadecimal number systems.

> **(type)**
> **(casting**
> **operator)**

Non-Literal Characters

All characters contained in a string enclosed in quotes (") or single characters enclosed in apostrophes (') are assumed to be literal except for characters preceded by a \. The following is a list of the special meanings of these characters:

\n   is replaced with a line feed character

\t   is replaced with a horizontal tab character

\v   is replaced with a vertical tab character

\b   is replaced with a backspace character

\r   is replaced with a carriage return character

\f   is replaced with a form feed character

\###   The ASCII character whose octal representation is ### (no leading zero is necessary if all three digits are non-zero).

\'   single quote (apostrophe) character

\"   double quote character

****   backslash (\) character

5

Compiler Directives

Comments /* */

Name

/*   */ (comments)

Format

/* commentary */

Purpose

Comments are notes the programmer has written, usually to explain the function of some code or to elaborate on a programming technique that may not be obvious to the casual reader of the source code. Since comments are ignored by the compiler, there is no memory usage penalty associated with them.

Usage Rules

1. Any material may appear between the /* that opens the comment and the */ that closes it; this includes carriage return/line feeds, blank lines, or other material. Nested comments are not allowed.

2. Standard c has no other rules regarding comments. Some c compilers require that a blank space follow the initial /* and a blank space precede the closing */. It is suggested you do so for readability, even if your compiler doesn't require it.

3. No semicolon appears at the end of the comment directive.

4. Comments can appear anywhere a space or a newline character can.

Defaults

None.

Example

Preferred usage for multi-lined comments:

```
/* This is a sample of a multi-line
 * comment in Standard c. Note how
 * a vertical row of asterisks helps
 * highlight the comment.
 */
```

Alternate usage for multi-lined comments:

```
/*This is a less popular style of
providing a multi-line comment
in c. This style leaves more white
space on the paper, but does not do
```

```
the same job of "blocking" off the
commentary from the program.
*/
```

Usage for single-line comments:

```
/* This is a single line comment in c. */
/* It is suggested that you line up    */
/* the comment start and end brackets  */
/* of single line comments for ease    */
/* in separating comments from code    */
/* when reviewing a program.           */
```

Exceptions

Not applicable.

Returns

Not applicable.

comment

#asm

Name

#asm

Format

#asm

Purpose

The #asm directive informs the compiler the statements that follow are assembly language, not c.

Usage Rules

1. #asm is not universally implemented on c compilers and is extremely compiler dependent. The methods of passing information back and forth between the host assembly language and c also vary from compiler to compiler.

2. In general, the assembly language statements that follow the #asm directive and precede the #endasm directive are not modified or manipulated in any way by the c compiler; they are simply passed through intact. This implies that a c compiler, at some point, outputs assembly language code. Therefore, the style of your assembly language programming (labels, mnemonics, and so on) should match that produced by the c compiler, if possible.

3. Some c compilers allow the use of other directives within assembly language code while others do not.

4. No semicolon appears at the end of the #asm directive.

5. The #asm command must begin in column 1; do not tab in to type the #asm command.

Defaults

Not applicable.

Example

One compiler's (c/80) usage:

```
if (sector == -1)
{
        fcb;            /* leave value of variable in HL */
#asm
        xchg            /* move HL to DE for BDOS */
        mvi c,35
        call bdos
#endasm
}
```

#asm

Exceptions

Vary from compiler to compiler. Consult your compiler's reference manual.

Returns

Also varies from compiler to compiler. Some compilers may assume the stack is returned unaltered, while others may not.

#asm

#define

Name

#define

Format

```
#define identifier expression
```

Purpose

The #define directive allows you to replace any occurrence in the program of an identifier or identifiers with a string expression or string "token" of your choice. It is useful for largescale replacement of information or values highly subject to change as well as values that are constant. This statement operates as a compiler directive; its effect is global (at least until an #undef statement appears). #define could be described as a simple text macro replacement directive.

Usage Rules

1. By convention, the identifier is entered in uppercase letters to make it stand out as a parameter or constant within the program code, while the #define and string expression must be lowercase (unless it uses an identifier from a previously #define. The use of an uppercase identifier helps the reader of source code separate global identifiers from local variables or identifiers. Exception: Many programmers use lowercase identifiers for macros like max or min.

   ```
   #define max(a,b) ((a)<(b) ? (b) : (a))
   ```

2. #undef is used to cancel the replacement invoked with a #define statement. A second #define using the same identifier, with no intervening #undef, results in a compiler error message.

3. Arguments may be used within the identifier and expression. They are substituted for when the expression is used to replace the identifier in the source code. Arguments are presented in parentheses immediately following the identifier (no spaces are allowed between the identifier and the parentheses). A complex expression should be enclosed in parentheses if operators or multiple data values are used.

4. No semicolon appears at the end of a #define directive, but the expression may contain semicolons if you desire. They will be treated just as any text character would.

5. The #define command must begin in column 1; do not tab in to type the #define command.

Defaults

None.

#define

Example

Preferred formatting:

```
#define MAX(a,b)     ((a) < (b) ? (b) : (a))
#define FALSE        0
#define TWO          2
```

$\longrightarrow$ tab over to align token strings

Alternate formatting:

```
#define MAX(a,b) ((a) < (b) ? (b) : (a))
#define FALSE 0
#define TWO 2
```

$\longrightarrow$ no tabbing; single space only

Exceptions

Substitution does not occur within quotes (string or char type constants).

Returns

Not applicable.

#define

#else

Name

#else

Format

#else statement;

Purpose

The #else directive is part of the #if/#ifdef/#ifndef/#else/#endif compiler directive set. The #ifdef and #ifndef directives control the set of program lines that are compiled if the original condition is matched; #else controls which program lines are compiled if the original condition is NOT matched.

Usage Rules

1. Any statement or group of statements may follow the #else directive. Each of these statements (up to a concluding #endif) are compiled only if the original condition (#ifdef, #ifndef) is NOT met. Syntax for statements between the #else and #endif directives is exactly the same as for any c statement(s).

2. #else is optional. If no statements are to be compiled when the original condition is not true, simply leave out the #else directive.

3. No semicolon appears at the end of an #else directive.

4. The #else command must begin in column 1; do not tab in to type the #else command.

Defaults

None.

Example

Preferred formatting:

```
#else
      for (i = 0; i < MAX; ++i);
#endif
```
⟶ indent statements from the directives so that the statements can be clearly identified.

Exceptions

#else is not necessary if no statements would follow it.

```
#ifdef LINE_LENGTH
      for (i = 0; i < LINE_LENGTH; ++i);
#else
      ;/* do nothing */
#endif
```

#else

would be written

```
#ifdef LINE_LENGTH
    for (i = 0; i < LINE_LENGTH; ++i);
#endif
```

Returns

Not applicable.

#endasm

Name

#endasm.

Format

```
#endasm
```

Purpose

The #endasm directive is used at the end of the assembly language code begun with an #asm statement (see #asm, page 100).

Usage Rules

1. See the notes under #asm above.

2. No semicolon appears at the end of #endasm directive.

3. The #endasm command must begin in column 1; do not tab in to type the #endasm command.

Default

None.

Example

One compiler's (c/80) usage:

```
#asm
      MOV A, L
      DCR A
      CALL.ROUTINE.
      MOV B, M
#endasm
```

Exceptions

See the notes under #asm, page 100.

Returns

See the notes under #asm, page 100.

#endif

Name

#endif

Format

#endif

Purpose

The #endif directive is used to mark the end of a conditional compilation begun with an #if, #ifdef, or #ifndef directive. Nonconditional compilation begins again with the statement following the #endif.

Usage Rules

1. Since nested use of conditional compilation is allowed, the #endif directive terminates the innermost conditional compilation group.

2. If no #if, #ifdef, or #ifndef directive appears to match the #endif, a compiler error message results.

3. No semicolon appears at the end of the #endif directive.

4. The #endif command must begin in column 1; do not tab in to type the #endif command.

Defaults

Terminates only the innermost #if.

Example

Preferred formatting:

```
#if SINGLE
#define ME      1
#define YOU     2
#endif /* SINGLE  */
```
          ↑_____ comment to indicate which #if loop you think you
                   are terminating.

Alternate formatting:

```
#if MARRIED
#define WE      1
#define THEM    2
#endif
```
       ↑
       └_____ no comment

Exceptions

A missing #endif in an #include file will not be detected when the file is exhausted; the preprocessor will continue and cut parts of the file which did the #include!

> #endasm
> #endif

#endif

Returns

Not applicable.

#if

Name

#if

Format

`#if constant-expression`

Purpose

The #if directive allows conditional compilation of statements based upon the value of the expression that follows.

Usage Rules

1. An expression value of zero results in the suppression of compilation of all statements that follow, up to and including the matching #endif directive. An expression value of non-zero results in the compilation of all code that appears up to the matching #endif directive.

2. The expression in the #if statement must evaluate to a constant that can be tested against a value of zero.

3. No semicolon appears at the end of the #if directive.

4. The #if command must begin in column 1; do not tab in to type the #if command.

Defaults

None.

Example

Preferred formatting:

```
#if (term + 1)
    printf("This is memory-mapped\");
#else
    printf("This is terminal I/O\n");
#endif
```
⟶ tab in for conditionally executed statements.

Exceptions

None.

Returns

Not applicable.

#ifdef

Name

#ifdef

Format

```
#ifdef identifier
```

Purpose

The #ifdef directive commands conditional compilation based upon the
fact that a previously defined identifier has been encountered by the compiler.

Usage Rules

1. If the identifier exactly matches a previously defined identifier (uppercase and lowercase letters must also match), the statements that follow
   the #ifdef directive will be compiled up to and including the matching
   #endif directive. If the identifier cannot be matched to a previously
   defined identifier by the compiler, the statements that follow are NOT
   compiled.

2. The #ifdef directive may be nested.

3. The use of an #else directive in conjunction with an #ifdef directive is
   optional (see #else, page 104).

4. No semicolon appears at the end of the #ifdef directive.

5. The #ifdef command must begin in column 1; do not tab in to type the
   #ifdef command.

Defaults

None.

Example

Preferred formatting:

```
char chan;
#ifdef PRINTER
        chan = 1;
#else
        chan = 0;
#endif
```

$\longrightarrow$ tab in to indent conditional code.

Exceptions

None.

Returns

Not applicable.

#ifndef

Name

#ifndef

Format

#ifndef identifier

Purpose

The #ifndef directive is a complement to #ifdef. It commands conditional compilation of statements if NO definition has been encountered for the identifier.

Usage Rules

1. If the identifier exactly matches a previously defined identifier (upper-case and lowercase letters must also match), the statements that follow the #ifndef directive will NOT be compiled. If the identifier cannot be matched to a previously defined identifier by the compiler, the statements that follow up to and including the matching #endif ARE compiled. This is exactly the opposite of the #ifdef directive.

2. The #ifndef directive may be nested.

3. The use of an #else directive in conjunction with an #ifndef directive is optional (see #else, page 104). It is suggested that you not use the #else directive with the #ifndef directive, since the same thing can be done more clearly by using the #ifdef/#else construct.

4. No semicolon appears at the end of the #ifndef directive.

5. The #ifndef command must begin in column 1; do not tab in to type the #ifndef command.

| #ifdef |
| #ifndef |

Defaults

None.

Example

Preferred formatting:

```
char chan;
#ifndef PRINTER
    chan = 0;
#endif
```

⟶ tab in to indent conditional code.

Exceptions

None.

Returns

Not applicable.

#include

Name

#include

Format

```
#include "filename"
#include <filename>
```

Purpose

The #include directive is used to command the compiler to include the source code contained in the filename specified.

Usage Rules

1. The source code is inserted at the place where the #include directive is encountered. When the end of file has been reached, compilation returns to the line following the #include directive. #include can be used within an included file (nesting of #includes is permitted, although there is a typical depth limit of 7 or 8 nestings).

2. The actual format of the filename varies widely depending upon which operating system the c compiler is run under. Enclosing the filename in quotes when operating in UNIX results in a search of the directory containing the user's source file first, then the standard sequence of standard directories; enclosing it in angle brackets (<filename>) results in the search for the file in only the sequence of directories. Since the filename format is variable, we suggest you make a notation here as to the rules governing your particular operating system and compiler. "-I" flags can be used to extend the list of directories searched to include the user's header directories (UNIX only).

3. No semicolon appears at the end of an #include directive.

4. By common practice, a file name with a period followed by an h (such as stdio.h) is known as a header file. Header files are traditionally used for standard functions or definitions used in multiple c programs. Common header files include:

   ```
   stdio.h        standard i/o library
   math.h         math function library
   string.h       string function library
   ```

   See Sections 7-10 for descriptions of the functions that appear in these libraries.

5. The #include command must begin in column 1; do not tab in to type the #include command.

Defaults

See rule #2 above.

#include

Example

Preferred usage:

```
#include <stdio.h>    /* library file for
                       * standard I/O
                       * functions.
                       */
```
———————————————————►
Use a comment to explain what is expected in
the file.

Exceptions

None.

Returns

Not applicable.

#include

#line

Name

#line

Format

```
#line constant
#line constant identifier
```

Purpose

The #line directive is used to assign an arbitrary line number to the source code line that follows, usually for the purposes of error diagnostics. #line is often used when a language generator creates c code, in order to relate the c code to the generator input that created it.

Usage Rules

1. The constant following the #line directive is assumed to be the line number for the source code line that follows.

2. If an identifier follows the constant, the current input file is assumed to be named by the identifier. This usage is helpful when doing error diagnostics on source files that have #include statements in them.

3. No semicolon appears at the end of a #line directive.

4. The #line command must begin in column 1; do not tab in to type the #line command.

Defaults

If no identifier follows the constant, the source code file remains the same as previously.

Example

Preferred usage:

```
#line 1 printf.c
        wrk = hrs * pay; /* this is line 1 */
        /* this is line after 1 of file printf.c */
```

Exceptions

Some compilers do not include this directive.

Returns

Not applicable.

#undef

Name

#undef (undefine)

Format

```
#undef identifier
```

Purpose

The #undef directive tells the compiler to forget any previous substitution created for the identifier using #define.

Usage Rules

1. Use of an #undef statement for a identifier which hasn't previously been defined results in a compiler error message.

2. The identifier in the #undef statement must be the same case as the identifier in the #define statement; an uppercase identifier is regarded as being different than a lowercase identifier.

3. No semicolon appears at the end of a #undef directive.

4. The #undef command must begin in column 1; do not tab in to type the #undef command.

| #line |
| #undef |

Defaults

None.

Example

Preferred formatting:

```
#undef        ENSIGN
```
⟶ tab over to align identifiers with #define identifiers.

Alternate formatting:

```
#undef COMMODORE
```
⟶ do not tab; single space only

Exceptions

None.

Returns

Not applicable.

6

Control Structures

break

Name

break

Format

```
break;
```

Purpose

The break statement causes the termination of the innermost while, do, for, or switch statement.

Usage Rules

1. Control passes to the statement following the while, do, for, or switch statement that was terminated.

2. The break statement causes the immediate termination of the control statement being executed. With the exception of the switch statement, where break is required to isolate the individual cases, the break statement's function causes an interruption of program control, and should be avoided, if possible. Programming that relies on the break statement to pass control to another section of code often does not result in the most elegant solution to a coding problem. A break to the nearest control construct is sometimes used by programmers if the intention and resultant action can easily be followed by someone reading the code, however.

3. Use of the break statement is required in conjunction with the switch statement to ensure that only the code associated with the desired case is executed (see switch, page 131, for examples).

Default

None.

Example

Preferred usage·

```
switch (ascii_key)
{
    case 1:    go_left(1);
               break;
    case 6:    go_right(1);
               break;
    default:   stay_here();
               break;
}
```

break

```
while (--place > 0)
{
    response = getch();
    if (response != '\n')
    {
    ungetch(response);
    break;
    }
}
```

Exceptions

None.

Returns

Not applicable.

break

case

Name

case

Format

case constant—expression: statement;

Purpose

The case statement is part of the switch control construct. It gives the programmer the ability to execute code dependent upon the value of the constant-expression.

Usage Rules

1. The constant-expression must evaluate to an integer number or be of a char data type.

2. Each use of the case statement within a switch construct must have a different value assigned to the constant-expression. Two or more cases that end up with the same constant-expression value cannot appear in the same switch construct.

3. The constant-expression for each case statement is compared to the value of the expression calculated in the controlling switch statement. A value matching the case's constant-expression results in the execution of statement(s) following the colon in the constant expression and up to the next break statement. A value that does not match the case's constant-expression results in the statement(s) being ignored and the next case or default statement examined.

4. The number of case statements that may appear in a single switch construction is limited to the number of integer values possible for the expression that appears in the switch statement. However, the compiler does not necessarily check to see if the calculated values are unique or exactly match the case statements you use. It is suggested you perform your own range and/or error checking in conjunction with use of the switch/case statements.

5. Cases need not be arranged in any particular order (hierarchical, or ascending value). The default case (see page 123) need not be the last case, but normally is by convention.

Defaults

None.

Example

Preferred usage:

```
switch(arg)
{
```

case

```
            case 'a':  printf("a is for almonds");
                       break;
            case 'b':  printf("b is for blueberries");
                       break;
            case 'c':  printf("c is for cucumbers");
                       break;
            default:   printf("That wasn't an a, b, or c");
                       break;
    }
```

$\longrightarrow$ note ordered cases, which make finding a particular one easy.

Exceptions

None.

Returns

Not applicable.

case

continue

Name

continue

Format

```
continue;
```

Purpose

The continue statement terminates the current pass through the innermost while, do, or for loop, and causes program execution to continue with the next iteration of the loop.

Usage Rules

1. When a continue statement is encountered, the current repetition of the innermost while, do, or for loop is terminated.

2. Execution always resumes with the increment portion of a for statement or with the test portion of a do or while loop.

3. Use of the continue statement results in the forced termination of the current pass through a program loop.

Example

Preferred usage:

```
for(loop = 0; loop < max; loop++)
{
    if(prime(loop))
          continue;          /* skip primes */
    calc(loop);              /* calc using non-prime */
}
```

Exceptions

None.

Returns

Not applicable.

default

Name

default

Format

```
default: statement;
```

Purpose

The default statement is used in conjunction with the switch statement and specifies the statement to be executed when none of the switch cases are matched.

Usage Rules

1. The statement(s) following the default statement are executed, in order, if no other matching case in found in a switch construct.

2. After the default statement has executed, control is passed to the statement following the default.

3. The default statement is optional.

4. For stylistic reasons (ease in finding and clarity of program logic), the default case is normally the last one in a switch construct.

| continue |

| default |

Exceptions

None.

Example

Preferred usage:

```
switch(arg)
{
        case 'a':  printf("a is for almonds");
                   break;
        case 'b':  printf("b is for blueberries");
                   break;
        case 'c':  printf("c is for cucumbers");
                   break;
        default:   printf("That wasn't an a, b, or c");
                   break;     /* not necessary, but... */
}
```

Options

None.

Returns

Not applicable.

do

Name

do

Format

do statement while (expression);

Purpose

The do statement is used to indicate a section of code to be repeated until the value of the expression in the while test becomes zero.

Usage Rules

1. The section of code that appears between the do and while statements is executed at least once, since the while test is always performed after the section of code has executed. See also while, page 132.

2. The section of code is repeated until the value of the expression becomes zero. Program control resumes with the statement following the expression.

Example

Preferred usage:

```
do
     {
          for( x =0; x =66; ++x )
               write(1,*line[x],65);
     }
while (keypress == 0);      /* end do */
```

$\longrightarrow$ comment to indicate end of do, otherwise reader of code might think this is the start of a while loop.

Exceptions

None.

Returns

Not applicable.

else

Name

else

Format

```
else statement;
```

Purpose

The else statement is used in conjunction with the if statement and defines program code to be executed when the if test evaluates to zero.

Usage Rules

1. When if statements are nested, the else statement is matched to the innermost if statement (the closest preceding if that has not already been matched with an else).

2. If an if construct appears without an else statement, no program code is executed when the if test evaluates to zero.

Defaults

None.

Example

Preferred usage:

```
if (curpos < width)
    ++curpos;
else
    curpos = 1;
```

$\longrightarrow$ indent program statements to show inherent if-else structure

Exceptions

None.

Returns

Not applicable.

`do`

`else`

for

Name

for

Format

for (initialization; test; incrementation) statement;

Purpose

The for statement defines a statement or set of statements that are executed repeatedly as directed by the conditions that define a program loop.

Usage Rules

1. 1. The initialization, test, and incrementation expressions are all optional. The semicolons must appear as placeholders when an expression is omitted. If the test expression is missing it is interpreted as being always TRUE (a break or other statement must terminate the loop or you have an endless loop).

2. The initialization expression is evaluated before any statements in the loop are executed. Generally, the initialization expression is used to set an initial value for a variable used in the test expression.

3. The test expression is evaluated before any statements in the loop are executed. If the expression evaluates to non-zero, the program statements in the loop are executed. Otherwise, execution of the loop is terminated and the first statement following the for construction is executed. The test expression normally uses a relational or logical operator (not =), although it is possible to use assignment operators. An example of this last point would be

```
for(i=10;a[i]=i;--i)
    ;
```

which terminates after a[0] = 0 is done.
Another test expression often found in c programs looks like this:

```
for (count = 0;(c=getchar()) != ' ';++count)
    do_something(c);
```

where the test contains a function call (getchar( )).

4. The incrementation expression is performed when a complete pass through the loop has been made. If the test expression evaluates to zero, the incrementation expression is not executed. In general, the incrementation expression is most commonly used to revalue a variable used in the test expression.

5. The for construct is equivalent to the following while construct:

```
initialization;
while (test)
{
```

```
statement;
incrementation;
}
```

6. The two semicolons within the parentheses must appear. The initialization, test, and increment instructions are optional. Use of the comma operator can be made to place more than one expression within the initialization, test, or incrementation portions of the for statement.

Defaults

If the test expression is missing, it is treated as being always TRUE (i.e., non-zero).

Example

Preferred usage:

```
for (loop=begin; loop>=min; --loop)
{
    makeline(loop);
    showline(loop);
}
```

Exceptions

None.

for

Returns

Not applicable.

goto

Name

goto

Format

goto label;

Purpose

The goto statement allows the programmer to force program execution to be transferred to the statements that begin at the identified label.

Usage Rules

1. The goto statement allows the programmer to avoid normal program structure and to hide the logical program flow. In most instances, use of a goto shows the programmer doesn't understand the logical sequence of the program statements; almost all use of gotos can be avoided by writing tightly structured code. Therefore, the goto statement is to be avoided, if possible. A valid use of a goto might be to terminate a program elegantly when it encounters an error condition deep within nested logic.

2. The label must be in the current function, and is an identifier with the following format:

   name:

   The label name must conform to the naming conventions listed on page 2.

Defaults

None.

Example

Usage:

```
main()
{
    goto here;
    printf("This never appears");
here:
    printf("This does appear");
}
```

Exceptions

None.

Returns

Not applicable.

if

Name

if

Format

```
if (expression) statement;
if (expression) statement; else statement;
```

Purpose

The if statement allows the programmer to define code that is executed conditionally when a certain condition is met.

Usage Rules

1. The expression is evaluated first. The expression must be contained within parentheses. If the expression evaluates to non-zero, the statement immediately following is executed. Otherwise, if an else statement is present, the statement following it is executed (see else, page 125). If no else statement is present and the expression evaluates to zero, execution resumes with the next statement following the if construct.

2. if statements may be nested; another if statement may appear as the statement to be executed if the expression is non-zero. An if structure is terminated by the first semi-colon (following the else, if present) if curly brackets are not used to show the structure.

3. If there is any ambiguity over which else belongs to which if, use braces to show the logical structure.

4. The else construct is detailed separately (see page 125).

Defaults

None

Example

Preferred usage:

```
if (isspace(c))
      putchar('\n');
else
      putchar(c);
```

→ indent statements to show the basic if-else structure

```
if (isspace(c))
{
      putchar(',');
      putchar('\n');
}      /* note: no semicolon after braces */
else
      putchar(c);
```

if

Exceptions

None.

Returns

Not applicable.

switch

Name

switch

Format

```
switch (expression) statement;
```

Purpose

The switch statement is used to direct conditional execution of program code based upon the calculated value of the expression.

Usage Rules

1. Any statement may follow the expression in a switch statement, but normally there are multiple case statements that follow.

2. The switch construct is terminated by either of the following:
   - execution of a break statement
   - encountering the end of the switch construct

3. The expression in the switch statement is evaluated normally, but the result must be of data type int.

4. See also case (page 120) and break (page 118).

switch

Defaults

The expression must evaluate to data type int.

Example

Preferred usage:

```
switch(c)
{
    case '\n':
    case '\r':
        putchar('\n');
        break;
    case '\t':
        place = place + 8;
        xpos(place);
        break;
    default:
        putchar(c);
        break;
}
```

Exceptions

None.

Returns

Not applicable.

while

Name

while

Format

```
while(expression) statement;
```

Purpose

Used to create a program section consisting of one or more statements that is executed only while a specific condition is met.

Usage Rules

1. The expression is evaluated before the statement is executed.

2. The condition is evaluated to a Boolean value of TRUE or FALSE, with the definition of FALSE being equal to zero and TRUE being non-zero. Be wary of relying upon an integer or bitwise interpretation of the expression, especially if the expression contains variable types other than integer.

3. Program flow continues with the statement following the while structure when the evaluation of the condition results in a FALSE interpretation. NOTE: The evaluation is performed BEFORE the body of statements are executed; thus, the while structure can be skipped if the initial evaluation is FALSE.

4. Make sure a value of FALSE (zero) can be generated, or you may end up with a program that endlessly repeats the loop.

Defaults

None.

Example

Preferred formatting:

```
while ((c = getchar()) != EOF)
    {
        if (isascii(c))
            putchar(c);
        else
            putchar('\n');
    }    /* end while */
```

⟶ comment shows which structure is being terminated.

Alternate (less readable) formatting:

```
while ((c = getchar()) != EOF) {
    if (isascii(c))
            putchar(c);
    else
            putchar('\n\);
}
```

while

Exceptions

Not applicable.

Returns

Not applicable.

while

7

Common stdio.h Library Functions

clearerr

Name

clearerr (stands for CLEAR file ERRor)

Format

```
clearerr(file pointer);
```

Purpose

The clearerr function clears any error indicator for the file stream indicated.

Usage Rules

1. ferror is used to find out whether an error has occurred. If ferror indicates an error has occurred, clearerr should be used to clear the error condition.

Defaults

None.

Example

Sample use:

```
if(ferror(fp))
{
        printf("Error number: %d",fileno(fp));
        clearerr(fp);
}
```

Exceptions

Not implemented on some compilers.

Returns

Not applicable.

fclose

Name

fclose (stands for File CLOSE)

Format

```
fclose(file pointer);
```

Purpose

The fclose function is used to cancel the assignment of the pointer to the file originally set up by an fopen statement.

Usage Rules

1. fclose should be called to close access to a file as soon as the file in question is no longer needed.

2. Using fclose frees the assigned pointer for assignment to another file, if desired.

3. The pointer used in the fclose statement must match a pointer set up by an fopen statement.

4. You should always check the returned value from fclose to see if an error occurred during the fclose operation.

5. fclose automatically flushes the buffer in which putc or related functions are collecting data.

clearerr

fclose

Defaults

fclose is automatically performed if a c program terminates without encountering any errors. All files are closed by the standard termination of a program. It is nevertheless recommended you use fclose to close files and not rely upon an assumed "good" termination. The penalty for not properly closing a file in some operating systems can result in as much as the loss of the entire file, although most operating systems would only lose portions of the file.

Example

Sample use:

```
int check;
FILE *pointer;
pointer = fopen("MYFILE","W");
      addtext(line);
check = fclose(pointer);
if (check)
      error_help;
else
      go_on;
```

fclose

→ If only a few lines appear between an open and close, it is good practice to indent the statements in between so that you can easily see what happens while the file is open.

Exceptions

None.

Returns

A -1 (non-zero) is returned if an error occurs during the file close operation; this indicates the file probably was not closed properly and the programmer should work under this assumption. A 0 (zero) is returned if the operation is completed successfully.

feof

Name

feof (stands for File End Of File)

Format

```
feof(file pointer);
```

Purpose

The feof function provides a means of testing whether or not the end of file has been read on the input stream.

Usage Rules

1. The file pointer should match the returned value from a valid fopen statement.

Defaults

None.

Example

Sample use:

```
if(feof(fp))
{
    fclose(fp);
    printf("End of File");
}
```

feof

Exceptions

Some compilers do not implement this function.

Returns

Returns a non-zero if the end of the file has been read from the stream; zero otherwise.

ferror

Name

ferror (stands for File ERROR)

Format

```
ferror(file pointer);
```

Purpose

The ferror function reports the error status associated with the file stream in question.

Usage Rules

1. The file pointer should be the returned value from a valid fopen statement.

2. The error indicator is set when an error occurs and is not cleared until a clearerr statement (see page 136) is executed. Do not assume an error has just occurred; it may have happened anytime between the fopen (or last clearerr) and your use of the ferror function.

Defaults

None.

Example

Sample use:

```
if(ferror(fp))
{
    printf("Error number: %d",fileno(fp));
    clearerr(fp);
}
```

Exceptions

Some compilers do not implement this function.

Returns

A non-zero is returned if an error has occurred; a zero is returned if no error has been detected since the last fopen or clearerr statement.

fflush

Name

fflush (stands for File FLUSH)

Format

```
fflush(file pointer);
```

Purpose

fflush causes all information about the file stream to be written from the buffer to the disk file.

Usage Rules

1. The fflush function is used to write all information about the stream (file data and file control information) to be written to the associated disk file. Normally, fflush is used periodically by a program to insure that no data is lost if the program or system crashes.

2. The file remains open after fflush is used.

3. The file pointer must be the returned value from a valid fopen statement.

Defaults

None.

Example

Sample use:

```
fflush(fp);
```

Exceptions

Some compilers do not implement this function.

Returns

Non-zero if the file was not flushed successfully; a zero if successful.

ferror

fflush

fgetc

Name

fgetc (stands for File GET Character)'

Format

fgetc(file pointer);

Purpose

The fgetc function reads a single character from the referenced file.

Usage Rules

1. fgetc behaves like getc, but is a genuine function as opposed to a macro.

2. The file pointer must be the returned value from a valid fopen statement.

Defaults

None.

Example

Sample use:

```
int *point;
point = fopen("FILE", "r");
if ((fgetc(point)) == \0)
      printf("We're at end of line");
```

Exceptions

None.

Returns

Returns the next character from the input stream as an integer value (with non-used bits filled with zeroes), an end of file character (-1), or a negative value if an error occurs.

fgets

Name

fgets (stands for File GET String)

Format

```
fgets(string,size,file pointer);
```

Purpose

The fgets function reads the next input line in the referenced file into the character array unless the line is longer than a user-specified size (the assumed length of the array string) in which case the remaining portion of the input line is truncated.

Usage Rules

1. The next input line is defined as being all characters up to and.including the next newline character (\n).

2. The fgets function reads the number of characters specified by the user less one (size - 1) unless fgets encounters a newline character, in which case input is terminated immediately following input of the newline character. Space is allowed for the \0 character. If a newline character is the first character encountered, only a null is returned by the function.

3. The string array that holds the returned characters is terminated by a null (\0).

4. The file pointer must be the returned value from a valid fopen statement.

Defaults

None.

Example

Sample use:
```
int line_length = 52;
char string[52];
FILE *pointer;
pointer = fopen("FILE","r");
if ((fgets(string,line_length,pointer);) == \0)
    printf("We're at end of line");
```

Exceptions

None.

Returns

The string or a null character (\0) if the current input point is at the end of a line.

fopen

Name

fopen (stands for File OPEN)

Format

```
fopen(filename,mode);
```

Purpose

The fopen function sets up the specified file for access by the c program.

Usage Rules

1. The fopen function returns a pointer to the file for later use by other file functions.

2. Filenames and modes may vary between operating systems and compilers. Check your compiler's manual for more information. Standard UNIX c allows the following ASCII modes: r, w, and sometimes a or u. Some operating system/compiler combinations allow binary file modes of rb, wb, and ub. The following table shows what happens in each of the modes based upon the original condition of the file.

mode	meaning	condition		action
r =	READ ASCII	file exists	→	file is opened for reading
		no file	→	null returned
w =	WRITE ASCII	file exists	→	file contents erased, file opened for writing
		no file	→	file created and opened for writing
a =	APPEND ASCII	file exists	→	file opened for writing
		no file	→	file created and opened for writing
u =	UPDATE ASCII	file exists	→	file opened for writing
		no file	→	file created and opened for writing
r+ =	APPEND ASCII	file exists	→	file opened for writing at end
		no file	→	file created and opened for writing
rb =	READ BINARY	file exists	→	file is opened for reading
		no file	→	null returned

fopen

mode	meaning	condition		action
wb =	WRITE BINARY	file exists	$\longrightarrow$	file contents erased, file opened for writing
		no file	$\longrightarrow$	file created and opened for writing
ub =	UPDATE BINARY	file exists	$\longrightarrow$	file opened for writing
		no file	$\longrightarrow$	file created and opened for writing

Defaults

fopen is not normally needed to use the stdin, stdout, and stderr files; these files are normally opened automatically by the operating system for c.

Example

Sample use:

```
FILE *point;
point = fopen("MYFILE","w");
```

Exceptions

Some operating systems restrict the number of files that can be open at one time. Some modes mentioned above may not be available on some operating systems.

fopen

Returns

A null pointer, typically all zeroes, is returned if an error occurs during the open function. A pointer (file descriptor) is returned if the file is opened successfully.

fprintf

Name

fprintf (stands for File PRINT Function)

Format

fprintf(file pointer,formatting string,arguments);

Purpose

The fprintf function allows the user to write formatted output to the specified file.

Usage Rules

1. The referenced file must be open before using the fprintf function.

2. The fprintf function uses the same string and arguments conversions
   as do printf (see printf and Appendix E for fuller descriptions; see also
   sprintf, a related function described on page 163). The only difference
   between a fprintf and printf is the fprintf function performs its work on
   a user-specified file, while the printf function always works with the
   stdout file.

3. The arguments must match any conversion requests in the string.

Defaults

None.

Example

Sample use:
```
int number = 123;
char letters[4] = "ABC";
FILE *fp;
fp = fopen("FILE","w");
fprintf(fp,"%3d %s   <-- SEE?", number,letters);
```

(this sends "123 ABC <-- SEE?" to the file)

Exceptions

None.

Returns

A -1 (non-zero) is returned if an error occurs; otherwise a 0 (zero) is returned.

fputc

Name

fputc (stands for File PUT Character)

Format

```
fputc(character,file pointer);
```

Purpose

The fputc function writes a character to the specified file. See related function, putc, on page 159.

Usage Rules

1. The file specified by the file pointer must have previously been opened by an fopen statement.

2. Good programming practice dictates that you examine the return from the function to check whether an error occurred during the write. Note: UNIX sometimes drops output without any form of warning if disk space is exceeded.

Defaults

None.

Example

Sample use:

```
FILE *inits
inits = fopen("FAMILY","w");
     char letter = "H";
     fputc(letter,inits);
fclose(inits);
```

fprintf

fputc

Exceptions

None.

Returns

A -1 (end of file) is returned if an error occurs; otherwise a 0 (zero) is returned.

fputs

Name

fputs (stands for File PUT String)

Format

```
fputs(string,file pointer);
```

Purpose

The fputs function writes a string to the specified file.

Usage Rules

1. The file specified by the file pointer must have previously been opened by an fopen statement.

2. The fputs function writes the string to the file specified up to, but not including, the first null character (\0) encountered.

3. Good programming practice dictates that you examine the return from the function to check whether an error occurred during the write.

Defaults

None.

Example

Sample use:

```
FILE *sisters;
char string[] = "mary reenie lizzie";
sisters = fopen("SISTER.DAT","w");
        fputs(string,sisters);
fclose(sisters);
```

Exceptions

None.

Returns

A -1 (end of file) is returned if an error occurs; otherwise a 0 (zero) is returned.

fread

Name

fread (stands for File READ)

Format

```
fread(buffer,size,number,file pointer);
```

Purpose

The fread function reads information from a file and places it in memory where the program may use it.

Usage Rules

1. "buffer" must be a pointer to a location to store the data that is read; "size" is the size of each data item to be read (in bytes); "number" is the number of data items to be read; "file pointer" is the returned value from a valid fopen statement and represents the file to be used for the read operation.

Defaults

None.

Example

Sample use:

```
FILE *slaves;
int *buffer;
int test, num, size;
slaves = fopen("file","r");
        test = fread(buffer,size,num,slaves);
        if (test == num)
                fclose(slaves);
        else
                _exit(); /* didn't read all */
```

fputs

fread

Exceptions

None.

Returns

The number of items actually read; zero if the end of file was encountered or if an error is encountered.

fscanf

Name

fscanf (stands for File SCAN Function)

Format

fscanf(file pointer,conversion string,arguments)

Purpose

The fscanf function reads information from the specified file according to the conversion string, and places this information into the arguments listed.

Usage Rules

1. The fscanf function is the same as the scanf function, except that fscanf gets its input from the programmer-specified file rather than the standard I/O. For a complete description of how this function works, see the scanf function on page 162 later in this section. See also sscanf, page 164.

2. The arguments must be pointers to locations where the input is to be stored. The conversion string must be enclosed in quotes.

3. Good programming practice dictates that you check the return code from the function to make sure no errors were encountered.

Defaults

None.

Example

Sample use:

```
FILE *point;
char letters[12];
int result, number;
point = fopen("MYFILE","r");
    result = fscanf(point, "%d %s", &number, letters);
fclose(point);
if (result != 12)
    printf("An error occurred.\n");
else
    printf("The number = %d, letters = %s.n",number,letters);
```

Exceptions

None.

Returns

The integer number of items successfully matched; a -1 (end of file) if an error occurs.

fseek

Name

fseek (stands for File SEEK)

Format

```
fseek(file pointer,number1,number2);
```

Purpose

The fseek function provides a method of altering the current read/write position in a disk file.

Usage Rules

1. The file pointer must be the returned value from a valid fopen statement; "number1" is the offset (in bytes) from the base and should be a long int on most systems; "number2" is a code indicating the base to which will be the offset.

   0 beginning of file (offset must be positive)
   1 current position in file
   2 end of file

2. Seeks to beyond the end of file should be avoided; depending upon the way the operating system handles such seeks, missing sectors or incorrect EOF markers may result.

Defaults

None.

Example

Sample uses:
```
fseek(fp,0L,0);   /* seeks first byte of file */
fseek(fp,-1L,1);  /* seeks last byte processed */
fseek(fp,0L,2);   /* seeks last byte of file */
```

Exceptions

Some operating systems do not keep track of the exact end of the file (specifically CP/M-80 and CP/M-86), which makes use of the base at end of file meaningless.

Returns

A -1 (EOF) is returned if an error occurs; otherwise the current position in the file is returned.

fscanf

fseek

ftell

Name

ftell (stands for File TELL position)

Format

```
ftell(file pointer);
```

Purpose

The ftell function provides a way of finding the current position in the file relative to the beginning.

Usage Rules

1. The file pointer must be the returned value from a valid fopen statement.

2. The position is returned in bytes from the beginning of the file.

Defaults

None.

Example

Sample use:

```
long jump, ftell();
jump = ftell(fd);
```

Exceptions

On some systems, the returned value is not in bytes. On such systems, the only way to tell where you are in a file is to perform a

```
result = fseek(fd,1L,-1);
```

and examine the result.

Returns

The current value of the offset relative to the beginning of the file, in bytes.

fwrite

Name

fwrite (stands for File WRITE)

Format

```
fwrite(buffer,size,number,file pointer);
```

Purpose

The fwrite function writes information to a file from memory.

Usage Rules

1. "buffer" must be a pointer to a location being used to store the data that is to be written; "size" is the size of each data item to be written (in bytes); "number" is the number of data items to be written; "file pointer" is the returned value from a valid fopen statement and represents the file to be used for the write operation.

Defaults

None.

Example

Sample use:

```
FILE *man;
int *buffer;
int test, num, size;
man = fopen("file","w");
     test = fwrite(buffer,size,num,man);
fclose(man);
```

Exceptions

None.

Returns

The number of items actually written; zero if an error is encountered.

getc

Name

getc (stands for GET Character)

Format

```
getc(file pointer);
```

Purpose

The getc function retrieves the next character from the indicated file.

Usage Rules

1. The file pointer must be for a file that has already been fopened.
2. The getc function differs from the getchar function by allowing the user to specify which file to get the next character from. See related function, fgetc, page 142.

Defaults

Most compilers automatically convert any char type input to integer; the return is considered an integer.

Example

Sample use:

```
int inchr;
while ((inchr=getc(fp)) != -1)
    add(inchr);
```

Exceptions

Since getc is implemented as a macro, getc usually results in unwanted side effects. An example of unwanted side effects results from

```
getc(*f++);
```

which, due to the repeated reference to the argument in the expansion, ends with multiple incrementations being performed.

Returns

The integer value of the character that was input; a -1 if the end of file or error occurred.

getchar

Name

getchar (stands for GET CHARacter)

Format

```
getchar()
```

Purpose

The getchar function retreives the next character from the stdin (standard input) device.

Usage Rules

1. ·Normally the getchar function gets the next character from stdin: console keyboard in most cases. However, if redirection is allowed by the operating system, the source may be a file if redirection has occurred. Getchar is the same as

```
getc(stdin);
```

Defaults

Some operating systems open the stdin device in the ASCII mode, which means an entire line is buffered in memory. In such instances, characters will not be available to the program through the getchar function until the next newline (or carriage return) character is entered.

getc
getchar

Example

Sample use:

```
#define EOF    -1
int character;
while ((character = getchar()) != EOF)
      process(character);
```

Exceptions

See defaults.

Returns

The positive integer of the character; a -1 for end of file or file error.

printf

Name

printf (stands for PRINT Function)

Format

```
printf(formatting string,arguments);
```

Purpose

The printf function writes formatted output to the standard output device. See also fprintf and sprintf, pages 146 and 163, respectively.

Usage Rules

1. The number of conversions in the formatting string and the number of arguments must agree or unexpected results will occur.

2. The formatting string must be contained in double quotes, and may contain "conversion characters" that allow the arguments to be formatted according to specific instructions. One indicates that a conversion character(s) is about to follow by using the percent sign (%).There are two types of conversion characters. The first (which appears last in the conversion string) specifies the type of output desired.

   d decimal notation

   o unsigned octal notation

   x unsigned hexadecimal notation

   u unsigned decimal notation

   c single character

   s string

   e floating or double number in decimal and exponential notation

   f floating or double number in decimal notation

   g the shorter (in character length) of %e or %f representations

   The second set of conversion characters is a modifier of the basic types, and must appear prior to the conversion type and in the following order (unnecessary modifiers should be omitted):

   - left justify the argument in the field

   n An integer number that specifies the minimum field length (extra spaces are padded with blanks unless a leading zero is used in the number, in which case zeroes are used for padding)

   . Separator. Separates the field length from the next integer constant, if present

printf

n An integer constant used to give the precision of the argument

l indicates the argument is of type long rather than type int or float

Obviously, the possibilities for the print formatting of even a single argument are many. Here are some examples to help clarify the possibilities.

argument = an integer, 123

format string	result
%d	123
%04d	0123
%o	173
%x	7B
%u	123
%-.012d	00000000123
%-12d	123_____

NOTE: underlines appear for blanks in these examples so the user can see different results more clearly.

argument = a floating point number, 12.34

format string	result
%f	12.34
%.1f	12.3
%06.1f	0012.3
%-6.1f	12.3__

argument = a string, ABCDEFGHIJKLMNOP

format string	result
%s	ABCDEFGHIJKLMNOP
%12s	ABCDEFGHIJKLMNOP
%-12s	ABCDEFGHIJKLMNOP
%.12s	ABCDEFGHIJKL
%20s	ABCDEFGHIJKLMNOP____
%20.12s	_____ABCDEFGHIJKL
%-20.12s	ABCDEFGHIJKL_____

printf

An explanation of the conversion characters is provided for you in Appendix E.

3. printf will attempt to convert arguments into the specified conversion type, but may get confused. Int to char, or vice versa, is one conversion that works. float to char does not convert correctly.

4. When there's a conflict between the field width specified and the number of characters in the argument, the portion with the larger number of characters to display is used.

```
string1[] = "ABCDEFGH";
string2[] = "ABCD";
printf("%6s %6s",string1,string2);

result: ABCDEFGH ABCD_ _
```

Defaults

None.

printf

Example

Sample use:

```
float pi = 3.14159;
int radius = 11;
char name[] = "THOM";
printf("The cross-sectional area at\n");
printf("%s's waist can be calculated by\n",name);
printf("multiplying Pi (%6.5f) by the\n",pi);
printf("square of the radius of his belly (%3d).\n",radius*radius);
```

Exceptions

Attempting to convert an integer into floating point notation (or any non-sensical conversion) results in an error. Various compilers exhibit the error in different ways, with most simply printing a nonsensical string for the mismatched specification (and possible others, as well) due to the problems of packing data from the argument list to a data type or size that is not consistent in size.

Returns

A -1 (end of file) is returned if an error occurs; a zero if no error happened.

putc

Name

putc (stands for PUT Character)

Format

```
putc(character,file pointer);
```

Purpose

The putc function writes a character to the specified file.

Usage Rules

1. The file descriptor should be the pointer obtained previously by opening a file.
2. Only a single character is written to the file by the putc function. Some compilers and operating systems may buffer output to files, meaning that no physical writing is done to the file until the buffer is full or the file is closed.
3. Good programming practice dictates that you check the return from the function to insure no error occurred during the process.
4. The character to be written may be of type char or int.

Defaults

None.

putc

Example

Sample use:

```
FILE *cabinet;
char response;
cabinet = fopen("DRAWER1","w");
    while((response = getchar()) != EOF)
        putc(response,cabinet);
fclose(cabinet);
```

Exceptions

Since putc is implemented as a macro, unwanted side effects sometimes occur. An example that produces unwanted side effects is

```
putc(c,*f++);
```

which, due to the repeated references to the arguments during expansion, results in multiple incrementations being performed.

Returns

A -1 (end of file) is returned if an error occurs; the character that was sent is returned if no error occurs.

putchar

Name

putchar (stands for PUT CHARacter)

Format

```
putchar(character);
```

Purpose

The putchar function writes the specified character to the standard output device (stdout).

Usage Rules

1. The putchar function is the equivalent of putc(character,stdout) and its usage generally follows that of putc (see above).

Defaults

The stdout device is used for the output.

Example

Sample use:

```
char letters[] = "ABCDEFGHIJ";
char *result;
for(result=letters; *result != 'J'; result++)
    putchar(*result);
```

Exceptions

None.

Returns

A -1 (end of file) is returned if an error occurs during the function; otherwise the character written is returned.

scanf

Name

scanf (stands for SCAN input Function)

Format

scanf(conversion string, arguments);

Purpose

The scanf function provides formatted input from the stdin device. See also sscanf and fscanf, pages 164 and 150, respectively.

Usage Rules

1. The scanf function uses the conversion instructions in the string (surrounded by double quotes) to place formatted data into the argument(s).

2. The arguments must be pointers to the locations where the input is to be stored. See Variable Usage in Functions, page 144.

3. Blanks (ASCII space), tabs (ASCII tab), and newline (\n) characters are ignored by the conversion process in the scanf function. Whitespace is only considered to be separate input items, unless a %c is used to grab an individual whitespace character.

4. An argument is filled either by all legally matching input characters (input numbers going into an integer argument, input letters into a string argument, and so on) up to but not including the next space, or, if a number of digits is specified in the conversion string, the number of legally matching characters that are specified. The function will not pass control back to the calling statement until either it has filled all arguments or an error occurs. Note: scanf treats spaces (blanks) as field separators, thus scanf is not very appropriate for inputting a line of text—use gets() instead.

5. The conversion string is formed similarly to that of the printf function. The following are legal conversion characters and must follow a percent sign to be recognized as such:

   d   decimal notation

   o   unsigned octal notation

   x   unsigned hexadecimal notation

   h   a short integer

   c   single character

   s   string

   f   floating or double number in decimal notation

   The d, o, and x conversion characters may be preceded by an l (a lowercase "L") to indicate a long rather than an int type number appears in the argument list.

putchar

scanf

scanf

Numbers may be used in the input formatting to indicate the number of places (digits) to expect in an argument. In this respect the scanf function works in the same way as the printf function.

The asterisk (*) character in a scanf formatting string means the next matching data type is ignored.

```
"%*d"     /* ignores next decimal number */
```

Any other character in the conversion string that is not part of a formatting command (percent sign followed by conversion characters), must be exactly matched by the next non-white space input from the stdin device or an error occurs.

6. Good programming practice dictates that you check the return from scanf to find out how many arguments were formatted or if an error occurred.

Defaults

Input is taken from the stdin device only.

Special Note

The arguments MUST be pointers or else the function will not work properly.

Example

Sample use:

```
do
        scanf("%4d %10s",&number,string);
while(number ! = 9999);
```

In the above example, the following results occur, based upon the input shown:

input	number	string
1234string	1234	string
123456string	1234	56string
9999string	9999	string

Exceptions

Some compilers simplify the function; some of the conversion characters mentioned above may not be valid.

Returns

A -1 (end of file) is returned if an error occurs; if not, the number of arguments formatted is returned.

sprintf

Name

sprintf (stands for String PRINT Function)

Format

```
sprintf(pointer,conversion string,arguments);
```

Purpose

The sprintf function is similar to the fprintf and printf functions, but formats a string in memory as opposed to a string being written to a file. See also printf, page 156, and fprintf, page 146.

Usage Rules

1. The pointer must be to the string in memory that will eventually contain the formatted output.

2. The rules for the conversion string and arguments are the same as for printf (see page 156 or Appendix E).

3. A null byte (0) is placed at the end of the string when the output is completed.

4. You must make sure the string used for the output has enough space to hold all the formatted characters created by the function. To this end, you can check the return from the function to find out how many characters were output to the string.

Defaults

None.

Example

Sample use:

```
char memory[50];
char string[] = "I forget small numbers like";
int number = 45;
int result;
result = sprintf(memory,"%s %d",string,number);
```

Exceptions

None

Returns

The total number of characters placed into the string, including the null byte (\0), are returned.

sscanf

Name

sscanf (stands for String SCAN input Function)

Format

```
sscanf(storage string,conversion string,arguments);
```

Purpose

The sscanf function reads information from a string in memory and formats it before placing it into the argument strings. See also scanf, page 161, and fscanf, page 150.

Usage Rules

1. The sscanf function performs in exactly the same way as the scanf function, with the exception that it takes its input from the storage string in memory rather than from the stdin device.

2. The arguments MUST be pointers to memory locations.

3. The conversion string specifications are the same as those of the scanf function (see above).

Defaults

None.

Example

Sample use:

```
char string[10],kite[10];
int number;
sscanf(string,"%10s %3d",kite,&number);
```

Exceptions

None.

Returns

The number of items successfully matched is returned; a -1 (end of file) is returned if an error occurred.

ungetc

Name

ungetc (stands for UN-GET Character)

Format

```
ungetc(character,file pointer);
```

Purpose

The ungetc function returns (pushes) the character back onto the input stream.

Usage Rules

1. The file pointer must be the returned value from a valid fopen statement.

2. The character pushed onto the data input stream will be the next character retreived by getc from that stream.

Defaults

Only one character may be pushed back at a time. Use of the fseek function makes the compiler forget any pushed-back characters still pending input.

Example

Sample use:

```
char test;
test = getc(fp);
if(test != '\n')
     ungetc(test,fp);
```

sscanf
ungetc

Exceptions

See defaults above.

Returns

Returns the character pushed back onto the input stream; a -1 (EOF) if any error is detected.

8

Common string.h Library Functions

index

Name

index (stands for INDEX string)

Format

```
index(string,character);
```

Purpose

The index function returns the first position at which the character is found
in a string.

Usage Rules

1. The index function only reports the first occurrence of a matching char
   acter within the selected string. Counting begins at zero (0).

2. If no matching string is found, a -1 is returned.

Defaults

None.

Example

Sample use:

```
#define EOF    -1
char line[80];
char letter;
match=index(line,letter);
if (match != EOF)
    printf("I found %c.\n",letter);
else
    printf("I didn't find %c.\n",letter);
```

Exceptions

Some compilers do not begin counting from zero. They return a positiv
integer representing the place of the first occurrence of the character withi
the string, or zero if not found. May be found under different names (strch
in UNIX system III and V).

Returns

The integer representing the place of the first occurrence of the characte
within the string; -1 if no match is found.

isalnum

Name

isalnum (stands for IS ALphaNUMeric character)

Format

```
isalnum(character);
```

Purpose

The isalnum function checks whether a character is a letter (alphabetic) or digit (numeric).

Usage Rules

1. Valid alnum characters are

   A B C D E F G H I J K L M N O P Q R S T U V W X Y Z
   a b c d e f g h i j k l m n o p q r s t u v w x y z
   0 1 2 3 4 5 6 7 8 9

2. The character to be checked must be of type char or must be an int (or convertable to an int) number representing a char.

Defaults

None.

Example

Sample use:

```
int result;
char testch;
result = isalnum(testch);
/* if result == 1 then testch is alphanumeric */
```

index

isalnum

Exceptions

None.

Returns

A 1 (non-zero) if the character is a member of the alphabet or a digit; a zero if not.

isalpha

Name

isalpha (stands for IS ALPHAbetic character)

Format

```
isalpha(character);
```

Purpose

The isalpha function checks whether a character is a letter (alphabetic) or not.

Usage Rules

1. Valid alpha characters are

   A B C D E F G H I J K L M N O P Q R S T U V W X Y Z
   a b c d e f g h i j k l m n o p q r s t u v w x y z

2. The character to be checked must be of type char or must be an int (or convertable to an int) number representing a char.

Defaults

None.

Example

Sample use:

```
int result;
char testch;
result = isalpha(testch);
/* if result == 1 then testch is alphabetic */
```

Exceptions

None.

Returns

A 1 (non-zero) if the character is a member of the alphabet; a zero if not.

isascii

Name

isascii (stands for IS ASCII character)

Format

```
isascii(character);
```

Purpose

The isascii function checks a character to see if it is part of the valid ASCII character set or not.

Usage Rules

1. The ASCII character set is considered to be

   0x00 through 0x7F   (hexadecimal)
   0 through 127   (decimal)
   000 through 177   (octal)

2. The character to be checked must be of type char or must be an int (or convertable to an int) number representing a char.

Defaults

None.

Example

Sample use:

```
int result;
char testch;
result = isascii(testch);
/* result == 1 means testch is ascii character */
```

isascii

isalpha

Exceptions

None.

Returns

A 1 (non-zero) if the character is part of the ASCII set; a zero if not.

iscntrl

Name

iscntrl (stands for IS CoNTRoL character)

Format

```
iscntrl(character);
```

Purpose

The iscntrl function checks whether a character is a valid control character (a character that performs a function as opposed to representing a symbol, letter, or number).

Usage Rules

1. Valid cntrl characters are

0x00 through 0x1F, 0x7F	(hexadecimal)
0 through 31, 127	(decimal)
000 through 037, 177	(octal)

2. The character to be checked must be of type char or must be an int (or convertable to an int) number representing a char.

Defaults

None.

Example

Sample use:

```
int result;
char testch;
result = iscntrl(testch);
/* if result == 1 then testch is control */
```

Exceptions

None.

Returns

A 1 (non-zero) if the character is a member of the control set; a zero if not.

isdigit

Name

isdigit (stands for IS DIGIT character)

Format

```
isdigit(character);
```

Purpose

The isdigit function allows the programmer to test a character to see if it is a number (digit).

Usage Rules

1. Valid digits are

   0 1 2 3 4 5 6 7 8 9

2. The character to be checked must be of type char or must be an int (or convertable to an int) number representing a char.

3. Do not assume a non-digit is automatically alphabetic (a letter). It could be punctuation.

Defaults

None.

Example

Sample use:

```
int result;
char testch;
result = isdigit(testch);
/* result == 1 means testch is a digit */
```

| iscntrl |

| isdigit |

Exceptions

None.

Returns

A 1 (non-zero) if the character is a digit; a zero if not.

islower

Name

islower (stands for IS LOWERcase character)

Format

```
islower(character);
```

Purpose

The islower function checks if a character is a lowercase character.

Usage Rules

1. Valid lowercase characters are

   a b c d e f g h i j k l m n o p q r s t u v w x y z

2. The character to be checked must be of type char or must be an int (or convertable to an int) number representing a char.

3. Do not assume a character that is not lowercase is automatically uppercase. The character COULD be a digit, punctuation, control character, or other non-uppercase character.

Defaults

None.

Example

Sample use:

```
char testch;
if(islower(testch))
     printf("Character was lowercase.");
else
     printf("Character was not lowercase.");
```

Exceptions

None.

Returns

A 1 (non-zero) if the character is lowercase; a zero if it is not.

isprint

Name

isprint (stands for IS PRINTable character)

Format

```
isprint(character);
```

Purpose

The isprint function checks whether a character represents a printable symbol, number, or letter (as opposed to a control character).

Usage Rules

1. Valid print characters are

0x20 through 0x7E	(hexadecimal)
32 through 126	(decimal)
040 through 176	(octal)

2. The character to be checked must be of type char or must be an int (or convertable to an int) number representing a char.

Defaults

None.

Example

Sample use:

```
int result;
char testch;
result = isprint(testch);
/* if result == 1 then testch is printable */
```

islower

isprint

Exceptions

None.

Returns

A 1 (non-zero) if the character is a member of the printable character set; a zero if not.

ispunct

Name

ispunct (stands for IS PUNCTuation character)

Format

```
ispunct(character);
```

Purpose

The ispunct function checks whether a character represents a printable symbol (not a control character or alphanumeric character). For example:

! @ # $ % ^ & * ( ).

Usage Rules

1. Valid punct characters are

   0x20-0x2F, 0x3A-0x40, 0x5B-0x60, 0x7B-0x7E   (hexadecimal)
   32-47, 58-64, 91-96, 123-126   (decimal)
   040-057, 072-100, 133-140, 173-176   (octal)

   [SPACE] ! " # $ % & ' ( ) * + , - . /   (representations)
   : ; < = > ? [\ ] ^ _ ' { ¦ } ~

2. The character to be checked must be of type char or must be an int (or convertable to an int) number representing a char.

Defaults

None.

Example

Sample use:

```
int result;
char testch;
result = ispunct(testch);
/* if result == 1 then testch is punctuation */
```

Exceptions

None.

Returns

A 1 (non-zero) if the character is a member of the punctuation set; a zero if not.

isspace

Name

isspace (stands for IS whiteSPACE character)

Format

```
isspace(character);
```

Purpose

The isspace function checks if a character is "whitespace" (invisible).

Usage Rules

1. Valid space characters are

0x09	0x0C	0x0A	0x0D	0x20	(hexadecimal)
\t	\f	\n		' '	(representations)
9	12	10	13	32	(decimal)
011	014	012	015	040	(octal)

2. The character to be checked must be of type char or must be an int (or convertable to an int) number representing a char.

Defaults

None.

Example

Sample use:

```
char incoming;
if (isspace(incoming = getchar()))
    putchar('\n');
else
    putchar(incoming);
```

ispunct

isspace

Exceptions

None.

Returns

A 1 (non-zero) if the character is a space; a zero if it is not.

isupper

Name

isupper (stands for IS UPPERcase character)

Format

```
isupper(character);
```

Purpose

The isupper function checks if a character is uppercase or not.

Usage Rules

1. Valid uppercase characters are

   A B C D E F G H I J K L M N O P Q R S T U V W X Y Z

2. The character to be checked must be of type char or must be an int (or convertable to an int) number representing a char.

3. Do not assume a non-uppercase character must automatically be lowercase; it could be a digit, punctuation, control character, or other type of character.

Defaults

None.

Example

Sample use:

```
int result;
char testch = 'T';
result = isupper(testch);
/* result == 1 means testch is uppercase */
```

Exceptions

None.

Returns

A 1 (non-zero) if the character is uppercase; a zero if not.

itoa

Name

itoa (stands for integer to ASCII)

Format

```
itoa(number,buffer);
```

Purpose

The itoa function converts an integer number into the corresponding string of ASCII digits.

Usage Rules

1. A leading minus sign is generated if the number is negative, otherwise the number is assumed to be positive (and no leading + is generated).

2. The minimum size of the buffer varies from compiler to compiler.

Defaults

The string is terminated with a null byte '\0', as standard in c.

Example

Sample use:
```
int number = 345;
char buffer[10];
itoa(number,buffer);
```

Exceptions

None.

Returns

The buffer pointed to in the calling statement contains the ASCII-coded string representing the digit.

isupper

itoa

rindex

Name

rindex (stands for Reverse INDEX string)

Format

```
rindex(string1,character);
```

Purpose

The rindex function returns the last position at which the character can be found in a string.

Usage Rules

1. The rindex function only reports the last occurrence of a matching string within the selected string. Searching begins at the last character; numbering of positions begins at zero (0).

2. If no matching string is found, a -1 is returned.

Defaults

None.

Example

Sample use:

```
#define EOF     -1
char letter;
match=rindex(line,letter);
if (match != EOF)
      printf("I found %c.\n",letter);
else
      printf("I didn't find %c.\n",letter);
```

Exceptions

Some compilers do not number the positions starting from zero; they start at one (1). They return a positive integer representing the place of the last occurrence of the character within the string, or a zero if not found. This function is found under different names on some compilers (strrchr in UNIX system III and V).

Returns

The integer representing the place of the last occurrence of the character within the string; -1 if no match is found.

strcat

Name

strcat (stands for STRing conCATenation)

Format

```
strcat(pointer1,pointer2);
```

Purpose

The strcat appends the characters of the second string onto the end of the first string and returns a pointer to the resultant string.

Usage Rules

1. The arguments to the strcat function are pointers to strings. The first argument is the pointer to the destination string. The second argument points to the string to be added to the destination string.

2. The destination string is not checked to see if it is large enough to hold the source string. If the combined strings are longer than the destination area, c will not detect this but will overwrite whatever follows the destination string. It is advised to use strlen or some other method of checking the string's memory space before using strcat.

3. A null byte ('\0') is appended to the end of the destination string upon completion of the concatenation.

Defaults

None.

Example

rindex

strcat

Sample use:

```
char namestring[30] = "Thom's ";
char *tostring = namestring;
char *addstring = "place";
strcat(tostring,addstring);
```

Exceptions

Note that no error checking is done by c to make sure the destination string is big enough to accept a copy of the source string.

Returns

Not applicable.

strcmp

Name

strcmp (stands for STRing CoMPare)

Format

```
strcmp(string1,string2);
```

Purpose

The strcmp function compares two strings and returns an integer result that indicates whether the strings were equal or one greater than the other.

Usage Rules

1. The strings must be correctly terminated by a null byte (0).

2. Identical strings are defined as those that have the same number of characters and matching characters, in order, up to and including the null byte.

3. The first position of disagreement is used to determine which string is greater than the other. If the first string is greater than the second, a value of greater than zero is returned. A value of less than zero is returned if the first string is less than the second. For example:

   "ABCDEFG"   is string1
   "ABCDEFH"   is string2

   ↑

   First character of disagreement. H is greater than G; therefore, string2 is greater than string1. Returns <0.

Defaults

None.

Example

Sample use:

```
char string1[], string2[];
int result;
string1 = "abcd";
string2 = "abc";
result = strcmp(string1,string2);
/* result is greater than 0 */
```

Exceptions

Some compilers have problems with characters not in the ASCII character set (i.e., greater than 127 decimal).

strcmp

Returns

A value of zero if the strings are equal (identical); a value of greater than zero if the first string is greater than the second; a value of less than zero if the first string is less than the second. The value is calculated by subtracting the ASCII value of the first mismatched character of the second string from the ASCII value of the same character in the first string.

strcmp

strcpy

Name

strcpy (stands for STRing CoPY)

Format

strcpy(pointer1,pointer2);

Purpose

The strcpy function copies the characters of one string to another string and returns a pointer to the resultant string.

Usage Rules

1. The arguments to the strcpy function are pointers to strings. The first argument is the pointer to the destination string. The second argument points to the source string.

2. The destination string is not checked to see if it is large enough to hold the source string. If the source string is longer than the destination area, c will not detect this but will overwrite whatever follows the destination string. It is advised to use strlen on the strings before using strcpy.

3. A null byte ('\0') is appended to the destination string upon completion of the copying.

Defaults

None.

Example

Sample use:

```
char *tostring;
char *fromstring = "purse";
strcpy(tostring,fromstring);
```

Exceptions

Note that no error checking is done by c to make sure the destination string is big enough to accept a copy of the source string.

Returns

Not applicable.

strlen

Name

strlen (stands for STRing LENgth)

Format

```
strlen(string);
```

Purpose

The strlen function returns the number of characters that comprise the indicated string.

Usage Rules

1. Characters are counted up to, but not including, the first null byte terminator (\0) encountered.

Defaults

None.

Example

Sample use:
```
int length;
char string[] = "#@$^%( *(^&@#) (%*@#$";
length = strlen(string);
```

Exceptions

None.

Returns

The number of characters in the string, not including the null byte terminator.

| strcpy |

| strlen |

strncmp

Name

strncmp (stands for STRing COMpare up to Number)

Format

```
strncmp(pointer1,pointer2,number);
```

Purpose

The strncmp compares two strings, character by character, until the number of characters specified have been compared. Returns an integer result that indicates whether the strings were equal or one greater than the other.

Usage Rules

1. The first two arguments to the strncmp function are pointers to strings. The last argument is a positive integer.

Defaults

None.

Example

```
Sample use:

int result;
char *string1 = "purty";
char *string2 = "purse";
result = strncmp(string1,string2,3);
/* everything checks up to the third pos */
```

Exceptions

None.

Returns

The first mismatched character (if any) of the second string is subtracted from the same character in the first string. A negative value is returned if the first string is less than the second string (the first mismatched character in the first string is lower in value than the second). A positive value is returned if the first string is greater than the second string. Zero is returned if the two strings match one another to the position specified.

strncpy

Name

strncpy (stands for STRing CoPY up to Number)

Format

```
strncpy(pointer1,pointer2,number);
```

Purpose

The strncpy function copies the second string into the beginning of the first string up to the number of characters specified and returns a pointer to the resultant string.

Usage Rules

1. The first two arguments to the strncpy function are pointers to strings. The last argument is a positive integer. The integer represents a maximum number of characters to copy (a null byte—\0—in the source string can also end the copying).
2. It is the user's responsibility to make sure that enough memory space is allocated to the first string to hold the resulting string.

Defaults

None.

Example

Sample use:

```
int result;
char *string1 = "cursor";
char *string2 = "purse";
result = strncpy(string1,string2,3);
/* string1 now is "pursor" */
```

strncmp

strncpy

Exceptions

None.

Returns

Not applicable.

tolower

Name

tolower (stands for convert TO LOWERcase)

Format

```
tolower(character);
```

Purpose

The tolower function changes any uppercase characters to their lowercase equivalent.

Usage Rules

1. Characters that are uppercase are converted to lowercase by tolower. All lowercase characters remain unchanged.

Defaults

None.

Example

Sample use:
```
char change_please = 'T';
change_please = tolower(change_please);
/* change_please is now 't' */
```

Exceptions

None.

Returns

The lowercase equivalent of the character.

toupper

Name

toupper (stands for convert TO UPPERcase)

Format

```
toupper(character);
```

Purpose

The toupper function converts lowercase characters into their uppercase equivalents.

Usage Rules

1. The toupper function makes any lowercase character into an uppercase character. Uppercase characters remain unchanged.

Defaults

None.

Example

Sample use:
```
char going_up = 't';
if (isalpha(going_up))
      toupper(going_up);    /* going_up now 'T' */
else
      printf("That wasn't a letter!\n");
```

Exceptions

None.

Returns

The uppercase equivaler.. of the character.

| tolower |

| toupper |

9

Common math.h Library Functions

abs

Name

abs (stands for ABSolute value)

Format

```
abs(number);
```

Purpose

The abs function is used to calculate the absolute value of a number.

Usage Rules

1. The number to be worked with must be an integer. The result is also an integer.

Defaults

None.

Example

Sample use:

```
int result, number;
result = abs(number);
```

Exceptions

The largest negative number allowed for an integer may not have a positive counterpart. This will give unpredictable results on non-one's complement machines.

Returns

The integer absolute value of the number specified.

acos

Name

acos (stands for Arc COSine)

Format

```
acos(number);
```

Purpose

The acos function provides the arc cosine of a number (in the range of 0 to pi).

Usage Rules

1. The number should be of type double. The returned number is a double.

2. The number should be expressed in radians.

Defaults

None.

Example

Sample use:
```
double result, number, acos();
result = acos(number);
```

Exceptions

None.

Returns

The arc cosine of the number; if the number is greater than 1, a value of zero.

abs

acos

asin

Name

asin (stands for Arc SINe)

Format

```
asin(number);
```

Purpose

The asin function provides the arc sine of a number (in the range of −pi/2 to +pi/2).

Usage Rules

1. The number should be of type double. The returned value is also a double.

2. The number should be expressed in radians.

Defaults

None.

Example

Sample use:

```
double result, number, asin();
result = asin(number);
```

Exceptions

None.

Returns

The arc sine of the number; if the number is greater than 1, a value of zero.

atan

Name

atan (stands for Arc TANgent)

Format

```
atan(number);
```

Purpose

The atan function provides the arc tangent of a number (in the range of
$-pi/2$ to $+pi/2$).

Usage Rules

1. The number should be of type double. The returned value is also a
   double.

2. The number should be expressed in radians.

Defaults

None.

Example

Sample use:

```
double result, number, atan();
result = atan(number);
```

Exceptions

None.

Returns

The arc tangent of the number; if the number is greater than 1, a zero.

asin

atan

atan2

Name

atan2 (stands for Arc TANgent of 2 numbers)

Format

```
atan2(number1,number2);
```

Purpose

The atan2 function provides the arc tangent of the first number divided by the second (in the range −pi to +pi).

Usage Rules

1. The number should be of type double. The returned value is also a double.

2. The numbers should be expressed in radians.

Defaults

None.

Example

Sample use:

```
double result, x, y, atan2();
result = atan2(x,y);
```

Exceptions

None.

Returns

The arc tangent of the first number divided by the second.

atof

Name

atof (stands for ascii to float)

Format

```
atof(string);
```

Purpose

The atof function converts a string of ascii characters containing digits in scientific notation to a double-precision floating point number.

Usage Rules

1. The string of ascii characters is converted to a double-precision floating point digit as follows:

   - Leading whitespace is ignored (space, new line, tab).
   - The sign (+, −), if included, must precede the digits.
   - Numbers up to a decimal point are assumed to be the integer portion of the number.
   - Numbers after the decimal point are assumed to be the fractional part of the number.
   - An 'E' or 'e,' followed by an optional sign and a sequence of digits, is assumed to be the exponent part of the number. A valid string:

   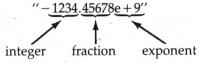

2. The precision available (the number of digits that may be converted and comprise the answer) varies from compiler to compiler.

Defaults

The function normally must be declared externally, since it returns a double number.

atan2

atof

Example

Sample use:

```
char string[] = "   -123.456e789";
double number, atof();
number = atof(string);
```

Exceptions

None.

Returns

The converted number, in double-precision floating point format.

atoi

Name

atoi (stands for ascii to integer)

Format

atoi(string);

Purpose

The atoi function converts an ascii string of digit characters into the equivalent integer.

Usage Rules

1. The conversion of the ascii string to integer number is done as follows:
   - Leading whitespace (tabs, new line, spaces) is ignored.
   - The sign (+ , −), if included, must precede the digits (some compilers do not accept the + sign).
   - Subsequent characters representing digits (up to the first non-digit character) are converted to an integer number. A valid string:

   "   − 12345"

   ↗   ↖

   sign   digits

2. The precision with which the conversion is done varies from compiler to compiler. Normally, atoi returns a long integer. If not declared, it will return a normal integer.

Defaults

If not declared as a long integer, the function returns a normal integer. The atoi function on most compilers does not detect overflow.

Example

Sample use:

```
long int number, atoi();
char string[] = "-1234";
number = atoi(string);
```

Exceptions

None.

Returns

The equivalent long integer or integer of the ascii string that was input.

atol

Name

atol (stands for ascii to long)

Format

```
atol(string);
```

Purpose

The atol function converts an ascii string of digit characters into the equivalent long value.

Usage Rules

1. The conversion of the ascii string to long number is done as follows:
   - Leading whitespace (tabs, new line, spaces) is ignored.
   - The sign (+, −), if included, must precede the digits (some compilers do not accept the + sign).
   - Subsequent characters representing digits (up to the first non-digit character) are converted to an integer number. A valid string:

   ```
   "    -12345"
   ```
   sign   digits

2. The precision with which the conversion is done varies from compiler to compiler. atol returns a long integer.

3. The string to be converted should be a pointer.

Defaults

None.

Example

Sample use:

```
long int number, atol();
char string[] = "-1234";
number = atol(string);
```

atoi

atol

Exceptions

None.

Returns

The equivalent long integer of the ascii string that was input.

ceil

Name

ceil (stands for CEILing of number)

Format

```
ceil(number);
```

Purpose

The ceil function provides the smallest integer value that is greater than or equal to the double number.

Usage Rules

1. The number to be converted should be a double within the integer range for the machine being used.

Defaults

None.

Example

Sample use:

```
int result;
double number;
result = ceil(number);
```

Exceptions

Unpredictable results occur when the double number to be converted to integer using the ceil function is greater than the range allowed for int values on the machine.

Returns

The smallest integer value greater than or equal to the double number.

cos

Name

cos (stands for COSine)

Format

```
cos(number);
```

Purpose

The cos function provides the cosine of a number.

Usage Rules

1. The number should be a double. The returned value is also a double.

2. The number should be expressed in radians.

Defaults

None.

Example

Sample use:

```
double result, number, cos();
result = cos(number);
```

Exceptions

None.

Returns

The cosine of the number.

ceil

cos

cosh

Name

cosh (stands for COSine Hyperbolic)

Format

```
cosh(number);
```

Purpose

The cosh function provides the hyperbolic cosine of a number.

Usage Rules

1. The number should be a double. The returned value is also a double.

2. The number should be expressed in radians.

Defaults

None.

Example

Sample use:

```
double result, number, cosh();
result = cosh(number);
```

Exceptions

In the case of numeric overflow, a "large" value is returned, the exact value varying from compiler to compiler.

Returns

The hyperbolic cosine of the number. See also Exceptions, above.

exp

Name

exp (stands for EXPonential)

Format

```
exp(number);
```

Purpose

The exp function provides the exponential value of the number input.

Usage Rules

1. The number should be a double. The returned value is also a double.

Defaults

None.

Example

Sample use:

```
int result;
double number, exp();
result = exp(number);
```

Exceptions

If the value to be returned exceeds the limits of the machine, a "large" value is returned. This value varies from compiler to compiler.

Returns

The exponential function of the double number entered. See also Exceptions, above.

cosh

exp

fabs

Name

fabs (stands for Float ABSolute value)

Format

```
fabs(number);
```

Purpose

The fabs function provides the absolute value of a number.

Usage Rules

1. The number should be a double. The returned value is also a double.

Defaults

None.

Example

Sample use:

```
double result, number, fabs();
result = fabs(number);
```

Exceptions

None.

Returns

The absolute value of the number as a float type value.

floor

Name

floor (stands for FLOOR of a number)

Format

floor(number);

Purpose

The floor function provides the largest integer less than or equal to the value of the number indicated.

Usage Rules

1. The number should be a double. The returned value is an int.

Defaults

None.

Example

Sample use:

```
int result;
double number;
result = floor(number);
```

Exceptions

None.

Returns

The largest integer less than or equal to the number being converted.

fabs

floor

log

Name

log (stands for LOGarithm of a number)

Format

```
log(number);
```

Purpose

The log function provides the logarithm of a number in base e.

Usage Rules

1. The number should be a double. The returned value is also a double.

Defaults

None.

Example

Sample use:

```
double result, number, log();
result = log(number);
```

Exceptions

None.

Returns

Zero if the original number was zero or negative; otherwise the logarithm of the number.

power

Name

power (stands for raise to POWER of)

Format

```
power(number1,number2);
```

Purpose

The power function raises one number to the power of another (exponentiation).

Usage Rules

1. The data type of the numbers used in the power function can vary from compiler to compiler. Kernighan and Ritchie provide an integer power function, but double data types are more likely.

2. The first number is raised to the power of the second number.

3. The second number cannot be zero in some implementations.

Defaults

None.

Example

Sample use:

```
int number = 5;
double power().;
printf("2 to the %dth is %f.\n",number,power(2,number));
```

Exceptions

Sometimes abbreviated as pow.

Returns

The result of raising the first number to the power of the second number. A zero is returned if the second number is negative or non-integral, or when both arguments are zero.

sin

Name

sin (stands for SINe)

Format

```
sin(number);
```

Purpose

The sin function provides the sine of a number.

Usage Rules

1. The number should be a double. The returned value is also a double.

2. The number should be expressed in radians.

Defaults

None.

Example

Sample use:

```
double result, number, sin();
result = sin(number);
```

Exceptions

None.

Returns

The sine of the number.

sinh

Name

sinh (stands for SINe Hyperbolic)

Format

```
sinh(number);
```

Purpose

The sinh function provides the hyperbolic sine of a number.

Usage Rules

1. The number should be a double. The returned value is also a double.

2. The number should be expressed in radians.

Defaults

None.

Example

Sample use:

```
double result, number, sinh();
result = sinh(number);
```

Exceptions

In the case of numeric overflow, a "large" value is returned, the exact value varying from compiler to compiler.

Returns

The hyperbolic sine of the number is returned. See also Exceptions, above.

sqr

Name

sqr (stands for SQuaRe of a number)

Format

```
sqr(number);
```

Purpose

The sqr function provides the square of a number.

Usage Rules

1. The number should be a double. The returned value is also a double.
2. sqr is the same as power(number,number). NOTE: Both numbers are the same.

Defaults

None.

Example

Sample use:

```
double result, number, sqr();
result = sqr(number);
```

Exceptions

None.

Returns

The value that results from squaring the number involved.

sqrt

Name

sqrt (stands for SQuare RooT)

Format

sqrt(number);

Purpose

The sqrt function provides the square root of a number.

Usage Rules

1. The number should be a double. The returned value is also a double.

Defaults

None.

Example

Sample use:

```
double result, number, sqrt();
result = sqrt(number);
```

Exceptions

None.

Returns

A zero if the number is zero or less; otherwise the square root is returned.

sqr

sqrt

tan

Name

tan (stands for TANgent)

Format

```
tan(number);
```

Purpose

The tan function provides the tangent of a number.

Usage Rules

1. The number should be a double. The returned value is also a double.

2. The number should be expressed in radians.

Defaults

None.

Example

Sample use:

```
double result, number, tan();
result = tan(number);
```

Exceptions

None.

Returns

The tangent of the number.

tanh

Name

tanh (stands for TANgent Hyperbolic)

Format

```
tanh(number);
```

Purpose

The tanh function provides the hyperbolic tangent of a number.

Usage Rules

1. The number should be a double. The returned value is also a double.

2. The number should be expressed in radians.

Defaults

None.

Example

Sample use:
```
double result, number, tanh();
result = tanh(number);
```

Exceptions

None.

Returns

The hyperbolic tangent of the number.

10

Other Common Library Functions

brk

Name

brk (stands for BReaK location)

Format

```
brk(number);
```

Purpose

The brk function sets the system's lowest location not used by the program (called the break location) to the number.

Usage Rules

1. The number must be a valid memory address.
2. Most compilers round the address up to the nearest boundary (usually 64, 256, or 512 bytes on most systems).
3. Any attempt to use memory above the break location results in a memory violation error.

Defaults

See point #2, above.

Example

Sample use:

```
int result;
address = &place;
result = brk(address);
```

Exceptions

See point #2, above. Some compilers do not implement the brk function.

Returns

A zero if the break was set; a -1 (EOF) if an error occurs.

calloc

Name

calloc (stands for Character ALLOCation)

Format

```
calloc(number,size);
```

Purpose

The calloc function is similar to the malloc function in that it allocates and initializes bytes of memory for temporary storage. The difference between malloc and calloc is that malloc allocates one array of bytes, while calloc allocates multiple elements, each of which contains an array of bytes.

Usage Rules

1. The calloc function provides a pointer to the start of memory, maintained like a stack (last-in, first-out) and initialized to all zeroes. The size of the memory area is calculated by multiplying the first number (the number of elements) by the second number (the size of each element) in the calloc argument list.

2. The size of the allocation buffer varies from compiler to compiler. The limits on the number of elements and size of each element varies from compiler to compiler.

3. Kernighan and Ritchie define two possible calloc and cfree functions. One is a stack assumed to use contiguous memory while the other is maintained as a list of memory areas released to the program by the operating system. Both Kernighan and Ritchie implementations return zero if the allocation request is bigger than the amount of remaining memory. In practice, you should check the returned value from calloc to see if the allocation was successful. Some implementations of c do not necessarily follow this standard; they might return an error message when no memory is available for the request.

Defaults

A zero is returned if the memory cannot be allocated correctly.

Example

Sample use:

```
char *calloc( ), *pointer;
unsigned int number1,number2;
if((pointer=calloc(number1,number2)) == 0)
{
    error("out of memory error.\n");
    exit(-1)
}
```

calloc

Exceptions

Calloc is a compiler dependent function. Check your c compiler's reference manual for further information.

Returns

The pointer is assigned to the first memory location in the block of memory that has been allocated for use. A zero is returned if the memory cannot be allocated correctly.

cfree

Name

cfree (stands for Characters FREE)

Format

```
cfree(pointer);
```

Purpose

The cfree function releases for use the block of memory that was allocated
to the pointer by the calloc function.

Usage Rules

1. The cfree function uses pointers previously assigned by the calloc function. Unexpected results occur if the pointer used in a cfree function
   does not match the pointer assigned by calloc.

2. The return code from the cfree function should always be checked to
   insure that the memory was freed correctly.

Defaults

None.

Example

Sample use:

```
char *pointer;
int number;
number = cfree(pointer);
if (number != 0)
{
    error("free memory error.\n");
    exit(-1);
}
```

$\longrightarrow$ Note check of returned number.

Exceptions

None.

Returns

cfree

A zero if the release of memory was completed successfully; a −1 if the
release was unsuccessful or if the pointer was unrecognized.

_exit

Name

_exit (stands for program EXIT)

Format

```
_exit(number);
```

Purpose

The _exit function terminates program execution without closing files or flushing buffers.

Usage Rules

1. No cleanup procedures are performed: Files are not closed and buffers are not flushed. Because of this, use of _exit should be reserved to cases where files must be left open (as in the case of the need to perform emergency manual maintenance).

Defaults

A value of zero should be the argument for _exit to indicate normal termination of the program. Non-zero values are used to indicate abnormal termination of the program.

Example

Sample use:

```
printf("This is the end...\n");
_exit(1);
```

Exceptions

None.

Returns

Program is terminated; there is no return. The value in the statement is normally passed back to the calling program.

exit

Name

exit (stands for program EXIT)

Format

```
exit(number);
```

Purpose

The exit function terminates program execution, closing files and flushing buffers.

Usage Rules

1. Open files are closed and data buffers flushed.

Defaults

A value of zero should be the argument for exit to indicate normal termination of the program. Non-zero values are used to indicate abnormal termination of the program.

Example

Sample use:

```
printf("This is the end...\n");
exit(0);
```

Exceptions

None.

Returns

Program is terminated; there is no return. The value in the statement is normally passed back to the calling program.

_exit

exit

free

Name

free (stands for FREE memory)

Format

```
free(pointer);
```

Purpose

The free function unallocates memory that was initialized with the alloc function.

Usage Rules

1. The free function returns the region of memory beginning at the pointer to "free" memory (memory that can be reused by the program). The pointer should be an address returned by the malloc function.

2. Normally, you should free memory in the reverse order in which you allocate it (UNIX allocates memory using a linked list, making this unnecessary). Failure to do this may result in corruption of the storage area and is not usually detected by the program.

3. You should always check the return of the free function to see that the memory was released correctly.

Defaults

None.

Example

Sample use:

```
char *buffer;              /* declare variable */
int number;
buffer=malloc(128);        /* allocates 128 bytes */
process();                 /* program code intervenes */
number = free(buffer);     /* we're done with the 128 bytes */
if (number != 0)           /* check return */
    abort( );
else
    go_on( );
```

Exceptions

None.

Returns

A zero if memory is released correctly; a -1 if memory is not released correctly.

malloc

Name

malloc (stands for Memory ALLOCate)

Format

```
malloc(number);
```

Purpose

The malloc library function allocates a region of bytes.

Usage Rules

1. The simplest malloc function provides a pointer to an area of memory maintained as a stack (last-in, first-out). Use of the free function (see page 222) to deallocate memory should be done in the reverse order of malloc.

2. The size of the allocation buffer varies from compiler to compiler.

3. The number argument should indicate the number of bytes to allocate.

Defaults

A zero is returned if the allocation could not be made.

Example

Sample use:

```
unsigned int size;
size = 1024;
char *memory;
memory = malloc(size);
```

Exceptions

malloc is a compiler dependent function. Check your c compiler's reference manual for further information. Some malloc functions initialize the allocated memory to zeroes, while others do not initialize the memory.

Returns

The pointer is assigned to the first memory location in the block of memory allocated for use. If the memory could not be allocated correctly, a zero is returned.

free

malloc

qsort

Name

qsort (stands for Quick SORT)

Format

```
qsort(pointer,number1,number2,function-name);
```

Purpose

The qsort function provides a method of quickly sorting elements in an array using the Quicksort algorithm.

Usage Rules

1. "pointer" is a pointer to the base of the array to be sorted; "number1" is the number of elements in the array; "number2" is the width (size in bytes) of each entry in the array; "function-name" is the name of a comparison function called with two pointers (to entries in the array), and must return the following:

negative integer (− 1)	if entry1 < entry2
zero (0)	if entry1 == entry2
positive integer (1)	if entry1 > entry2

Defaults

None.

Example

Sample use:

```
int *buffer;
int elements;

qsort(buffer,elements,sizeof(int),compare);

compare(s,t)    /* compare for qsort function */
char *s, *t;
{
    return strcmp(s,t);
}
```

Exceptions

Some compilers restrict the number of elements that may be sorted.

Returns

Not applicable.

rand

Name

rand (stands for RANDom number)

Format

```
rand( );
```

Purpose

The rand function provides a method of generating a pseudo-random number.

Usage Rules

1. rand normally returns pseudo-random numbers as integers in the range 0 to $(2^{15} - 1)$.

Defaults

None.

Example

Sample use:

```
int ann;
ann = rand( );
```

Exceptions

Some compilers return a different range of numbers, depending upon the bit size of the integer values used and the method used to calculate the random number.

Returns

A pseudo-random integer number.

qsort

rand

realloc

Name

realloc (stands for REALLOCate)

Format

```
realloc(pointer,size);
```

Purpose

The realloc function increases or decreases the size of a block of memory previously allocated with malloc or calloc.

Usage Rules

1. The pointer must be to the block of memory to be reallocated. The size must be stated in bytes.

Defaults

None.

Example

Sample use:

```
int *point,*result;
int size;
...
result = realloc(point,size);
```

Exceptions

Some compilers do not implement this function. The block of memory in the new allocation may be at a different address than the original. Reallocation can mess up data structures that contain pointers (as in linked lists).

Returns

The address of the new block of memory allocated; zero if the request could not be honored.

rand

Name

srand (stands for Seeded RANDom number)

Format

```
srand(number);
```

Purpose

The srand function provides a method of generating a random number using a seed value.

Usage Rules

1. srand normally returns random numbers as integers in the range 0 to $(2^{15} - 1)$.

2. An integer seed value is used to generate the random number. A seed value of 1 reinitializes the random number sequence.

Defaults

None.

Example

Sample use:

```
int anynum, seed;
anynum = srand(seed);
```

Exceptions

Some compilers return a different range of numbers, depending upon the bit size of the integer values used and the method used to calculate the random number.

Returns

A random integer number.

realloc

srand

unlink

unlink

Name

unlink (stands for UNLINK file from directory)

Format

```
unlink(filename);
```

Purpose

The unlink function removes a directory entry for the named file.

Usage Rules

1. The filename must be a pointer to the name of an existing file on the disk, and the referenced file should not be currently open.

Defaults

None.

Example

Sample use:
```
char[ ] file = "it";
unlink(file);
```

Exceptions

In UNIX, you may not unlink a directory.

Returns

A zero if the file was successfully removed from the disk; a −1 (EOF) if an error occurred.

11

Appendices

Appendix A—Bibliography

Books on the c language

Feuer, Alan R.: *The c Puzzle Book*. Prentice-Hall, 1982. This book is basically a workbook of puzzles involving the syntax of the c language, complete with annotated answers. Invaluable for testing one's c programming savvy.

Hancock, Les and Krieger, Morris: *The c Primer*. Byte Books (McGraw-Hill), 1982. An introduction to most of the c programming language. Features clear examples.

Kernighan, Brian W. and Ritchie, Dennis: *The c Programming Language*. Prentice-Hall, 1978. The first introductory book on c. Generally regarded as providing the definitive definition of what c is and isn't.

Kochan, Steven: *Programming in C*. Hayden, 1983. One of the most thorough of the introduction-to-c books available.

Plum, Thomas: *c Programming Standards and Guidelines: Version U (UNIX & Offspring)*. Plum Hall, 1982. A programmer's manual that attempts to provide guidelines for writing portable and correct c program code. A great number of specific lexical rules for formatting program code are provided.

Plum, Thomas: *Learning to Program in c*. Plum Hall, 1983. Originally conceived as a text for c programming seminars, this introduction has a strong emphasis on portable programming practices.

Purdum, Jack: *c Programming Guide*. Que Corporation, 1983. An introduction to the c programming language. This book has little or no UNIX bias, having been written by an implementor of a microcomputer version of c (Ecosoft c, for CP/M-based Z80 microcomputers).

Wortman, L.A. and Sidebottom T.C.: *C Programming Tutor*. Brady Communications Company, 1984. A companion book to this one, designed to teach the novice the c programming language.

Zahn, C.T.: *c Notes: A Guide to the c Programming Language*. Yourdon Press, 1979. Basically an expansion of the reference section of Kernighan and Ritchie, this book provides a formal definition for the c language.

Books with some applicability to c

Banahan, Mike and Rutter, Andy: *The UNIX Book*. John Wiley & Sons, 1983. Discusses c as it appears in the UNIX environment.

Dwyer, Thomas A. and Critchfield, Margot: *CP/M and the Personal Computer*. Addison-Wesley, 1983. A section on how to use BDS c on a CP/M based computer is included in the book, along with a summary of the c language.

miscellaneous: *UNIX Programmer's Manual, Volume 1*. Holt, Rinehart and Winston, 1979, 1983. A complete system manual for UNIX; has some references to files that are applicable to c programmers.

miscellaneous: *Unix Programmer's Manual, Volume 2.* Holt, Rinehart and Winston, 1979, 1983. A compendium of papers relating to UNIX and c. Of particular interest are the articles on lint (a program checker), make (a maintenance program), how to program with the UNIX I/O library, tours through the UNIX c compiler and a portable c compiler, and an article on the ADB program debugger.

Selected magazine articles about c

Anderson, Bruce: "Type Syntax in the Language c," *ACM Sigplan Notices,* Volume 15, #3, page 21. Discusses vague and lax tendencies of c syntax.

Barach, David R. and Taenzer, David H.: "A Technique for Finding Storage Allocation Errors in c-Language Programs," *ACM Sigplan Notices,* Volume 17, No. 5, p. 16. Description of a software tool for diagnosing errors in c programs.

Bolton, Bill: "Some Useful c Time Functions," *Dr. Dobb's Journal,* August 1981, p. 16. Time and date functions are presented.

Cain, Ron: "A Small-c Compiler for the 8080's," *Dr. Dobb's Journal,* May 1980, p. 5. Source code for the original small-c compiler.

Cain, Ron: "Runtime Library for the Small-c Compiler," *Dr. Dobb's Journal,* September 1980, p. 4. Source code for a runtime library for the small-c compiler.

Christensen, Ward: "Full Screen Program Editors For CP/M-80: Ed Ream's Editor in c," *Lifelines,* October 1982, p. 43. A review of Ed Ream's public domain editor, written in c (see below).

Cotton, G.: "A Master Disk Directory," *Interface Age,* November 1981, p. 162. A small-c program for a master disk directory utility.

Derfler, Frank: "Lattice c Compiler," *InfoWorld ReportCard,* Volume 2, Number 1, p. 76. A reprint of an *InfoWorld* software review of the Lattice c Compiler (IBM PC version).

Fiedler, David: "The BDS c Compiler," *Microsystems,* September/October 1981, p. 30. A review of the BDS c compiler, including comparison timings with UNIX versions of c.

Fitzhorn, Patrick and Johnson, Gearold: "c: Toward a Concise Syntactic Definition," *ACM Sigplan Notices,* Volume 16, Number 12, p. 14. A syntactical definition of the c language. An update of the article appears in *Sigplan Notices,* Volume 17, Number 8, p. 89, and uses Backus-Naur-Form descriptions of the c language.

French, Donald: "Statements, Operators, and Control Structures in c," *Electronic Design,* May 26, p. 165. An introduction to the c language with an emphasis on how it might help in getting new hardware running faster.

French, Donald: "Procedures and Pointers give c Extra Flexibility," *Electronic Design,* June 23, 1983, p. 143. A continuation of French's previous article.

Feuer, Alan and Gehani, Narain: "A Comparison of the Programming Languages c and Pascal," *ACM Computing Surveys,* Vol. 14, No. 1, p. 73. Conclusions about which language is better for which tasks.

Garrett, Roger C.: "Structured English for 'c' Programmers," *Interface Age,* October 1981, p. 30. An extension to the c language to allow structured English-like programming, called c.Plus. First of three parts.

Garrett, Roger C.: "More on 'c' Programming," *Interface Age*, November 1981, p. 26. The second article in the series on c.Plus (see above).

Garrett, Roger C.: "c.Plus (Conclusion)," *Interface Age*, December 1981, p. 34. The conclusion of the series on c.Plus (see above). Includes source code of extensions to c langauge.

Gerwitz, David: "An Introduction to the c Programming Language (Part I)," *Microsystems*, November/December 1981, p. 20. The beginning of an extended introduction to the language, including reviews of four c compilers: BDS c, Small-c, tiny-c, and Whitesmiths c.

Gerwitz, David: "An Introduction to the c Programming Language (Part II)," *Microsystems*, January/February 1982, p. 50. A continuation of Gerwitz's introduction to the language, with extensive test results for BDS c, Small-c, tiny-c 2, and Whitesmiths c.

Gerwitz, David: "Two More c Compilers," *Microsystems*, November/December 1982, p. 83. A comparative review of Aztec c II and Software Toolworks c/80 compilers. Includes BDOS function for CP/M written in c/80.

Gibson, T. and Guthery, S.B.: "Structured Programming, c and tiny-c," *Dr. Dobb's Journal*, May 1980, p. 30. A comparison of tiny-c with the c language, as well as several structured programming examples.

Gilbreath, Jim and Gilbreath, Gary: "Eratosthenes Revisited: Once More Through the Sieve," *Byte*, January 1983, p. 283. The Eratosthenes sieve benchmark written in c and tested on a number of c compilers.

Halfant, Matthew: "Small-c for the 9900," Dr. Dobbs Journal, July 1982, p. 66. A version of Small-c code generator for the Texas Instruments 9900 microprocessor. Based upon Small-c, version 1.

Hancock, Les: "Growing, Pruning, and Climbing Binary Trees with tiny-c," *Dr. Dobb's Journal*, May 1979, p. 37. Binary tree data structures are shown in a programming example that describes complex data interactions and extensive use of pointers.

Hendrix, J.E.: "Small-c Compiler, V.2," *Dr. Dobb's Journal*, December 1982. An update of the Small-c compiler source code, featuring a number of additions and corrections to the original code. The listing continues in the January 1983 issue.

Hendrix, J.E.: "Small-c Expression Analyzer", *Dr. Dobb's Journal*, December 1981, p. 40. A set of patches to the Small-c expression analyzer that corrects address arithmetic problems with the original compiler.

Hinsch, Hanno: "Five c Language Compilers," *PC Magazine*, February 1983, p. 210. Reviews of Intellect Associates C88, c-systems c, Computer Innovations C86, Telecon c, and Supersoft c, all for the IBM PC.

Howard, Alan D.: "Enhancing the c Screen Editor," *Dr. Dobb's Journal*, May 1983, p. 38. Additions and changes to the c Screen Editor by Edward Ream (see below).

Hughes, Phil: "BASIC, Pascal or tiny-c? A Simple Benchmarking Comparison," *Byte*, October 1981, p. 372.

Johannson, Jan-Henrik:, "Argc and Argv for Small-c," *Dr. Dobb's Journal*, December 1982, p. 62.

Kern, Christopher: "User's Look at Tiny-c," *Byte*, December 1979, p. 196. A review of the tiny-c interpreter/compiler.

Kern, Christopher: "printf for the c function library," *Byte*, May 1981, p. 430. A suggested printf function for c compilers that don't come with one.

Kern, Christopher: "BDS c Compiler," *Byte*, June 1981, p. 356. A review of the BDS c Compiler.

Krieger, Morris and Plauger, P.J.: "c's Grip on Hardware Makes Sense for Small Computers," *Electronics*, May 8, 1980, p. 129. Discusses how c fits between assembly and high-level languages.

Kvaleberg, Egil: "Small-c DISKDOC: A Repair and·Maintenance Utility," *Dr. Dobb's Journal*, April 1982, p. 26. Small-c source code for a CP/M disk repair and maintenance program.

McKeon, Brian: "A Small-c Operating System," *Dr. Dobb's Journal*, March 1983, p. 36. A simple operating system written in Small-c.

Madden, Gregory J.: "c: A Language for Microprocessors?" *Byte*, October 1977, p. 130. An introduction to the c language.

Mohler, Lorin: "A Disk Alignment Routine," *Microsystems*, November/December 1981, p. 70. Tarbell disk controller alignment routine written in BDS c.

Norris, Bill: "c-Bits (All About BDS c Version 1.45)," *Lifelines*, February 1982, p. 37. This article details new features of BDS c version 1.45.

Pugh, Tim: "BDS c, A Full Compiler from Lifeboat Associates," *InfoWorld*, March 31, 1980. A review of the BDS c compiler for CP/M systems.

Ream, Edward K.: "Ed2 - A file editor in c," *Dr. Dobb's Journal*, January 1982, p. 18. A simple file editor written in Small-c.

Ream, Edward K.: "A Better Screen Editor, Part 1," *Dr. Dobb's Journal*, July 1983, p. 34. A rewrite of Ream's original, with improved buffer handling.

Reid, Larry and McKinlay, Andrew: "Whitesmiths c Compiler," *Byte*, January 1983, p. 330. An extensive review of the Whitesmiths c compiler for the CP/M and CDOS operating systems.

Ritchie, Dennis, Johnson, S.C., Lesk, M.E., and Kernighan, B.W.: "The c Programming Language," *Bell System Technical Journal*, Volume 57 Number 6, p. 1991. The original public description of the c language by those responsible for creating and maintaining it.

Rodwell, Peter: "A Look at c," *Personal Computer World*, April 1983, p. 128. A British introduction to the language and review/examples using Software Toolworks c/80 compiler.

Skjellum, Anthony: "Argum—A 'c' Command Line Processor," *Dr. Dobb's Journal*, August 1982, p. 10. A function that simplifies parsing of command line instructions passed to a c program.

Skjellum, Anthony: "Using c Instead of Assembly Language," *Microsystems*, September/October 1982, p. 33. An argument that c can replace assembly language for many programming tasks.

Taylor, Jeff: "LIST—A Source-Listing Program for the c Language," *Byte*, June 1981, p. 234. A utility listing program written in c.

c Compilers for microcomputers

Product	Operating Systems
Computer Innovations	c86
10 Mechanic Street	MS-DOS, CP/M-86
Suite J-104	
Red Bank, NJ 07701	
201-530-0995	

Product	Operating Systems
Manx Software Systems Box 55 Shrewsbury, NJ 07701 201-530-7997	Manx c MS-DOS, CP/M-86, CP/M-80, Apple, TRSDOS, Atari, Commodore
Digital Research POB 579 160 Central Ave. Pacific Grove, CA 93950 408-646-6230	DR c CP/M-86, MS-DOS, CP/M-68K
Ecosoft POB 68602 Indianapolis, IN 46268 317-255-6476	ECO-c CP/M-80
Control-c Software 6441 SW Canyon Court Portland, OR 97221 503-292-8842	c86 CP/M-86
c Ware 1607 New Brunswick Ave. Sunnyvale, CA 94087 408-736-6905	DeSmet c CP/M-86
Microsoft 10700 Northrup Way Bellevue, WA 98008 206-828-8080	Microsoft (Lattice) c CP/M-86, MS-DOS
Supersoft POB 1628 Champaign, IL 61820 217-359-2112	Supersoft c CP/M-86, MS-DOS, CP/M-80
Telecon Systems 1155 Meridian Ave. Suite 218 San Jose, CA 95125 408-275-1659	Telecon c CP/M-80, MS-DOS, CP/M-86, Flex, Uniflex, RT-11, RSX-11
Whitesmiths 97 Lowell Road Concord, MA 01742 617-369-8499	c CP/M-80, MS-DOS, RT-11, UNIX
c-Systems POB 3253 Fullerton, CA 92634 714-637-5362	c MS-DOS, CP/M-86
Caprock Systems POB 13814 Arlington, TX 76013 817-261-4493	Small-c MS-DOS

Product	Operating Systems
Vandata 17544 Midvale Ave. N Suite 107 Seattle, WA 98133 206-542-7611	c CP/M-80
Quantum Software Systems 7219 Shea Ct. San Jose, CA 95139 408-629-9402	Quantum c QNX
Unipress Software 1164 Raritan Ave. Highland Park, NJ 08904 201-985-8000	c MS-DOS
Mark Williams Company 1430 West Wrightwood Chicago, IL 60614 312-472-6659	Mark Williams' c CP/M-86, MS-DOS, Oasis, Coherent
Software Toolworks 15233 Ventura Blvd. #1118 Sherman Oaks, CA 91403 213-986-4885	c/80 CP/M-80
LSI Japan Co. POB 508 Santa Clara, CA 95062	LSI c CP/M-80
tiny-c Associates Holmdel, NJ	tiny-c CP/M-80
Alcyon Corporation San Diego, CA	Alcyon c UNIX
Relational Software Menlo Park, CA.	Relational c IBM

User's Groups

Uni-ops POB 5182 Walnut Creek, CA 94596	/usr/group POB 8570 Stanford, CA 94035
Usenix POB 7 El Cerrito, CA 94530 415-528-8649	c Users' Group POB 287 Yates Center, KS 66783 316-625-3554

Appendix B—Assembly Language in c

Assembly language capabilities vary among c compilers. The following is a general discussion of how one microcomputer version of c (c/80) uses assembly language statements. Other microcomputer versions of c will probably work similarly; UNIX users should consult their manuals for the subroutine calling sequence, since the processor used will directly affect the assembly language call process.

Probably the first consideration to take into account is the format of the assembly language your c compiler uses. To cite one example, Software Toolworks c/80 comes with an assembler, AS.COM, which only accepts uppercase characters as input. On some processors, most notably the Z80, the style of mnemonics and pseudo operators can vary quite dramatically between assemblers. Some c compilers allow assembly and linkage using tools from other software creators, most notably Microsoft (M80 assembler and L80 linker).

There are basically two concerns in putting in-line assembly language code into a c program: passing of parameters and the labeling requirements for external routines.

On microcomputers, passing parameters usually takes place through the use of the stack or registers. The top of the stack is normally the return address (the address to have execution return to when use of the assembly language routine is finished). Any parameters that were passed to the assembly language routine will be next on the stack, in the reverse order of their declaration.

For example, here's some c/80 code to call a CP/M BDOS function through assembly language.

```
bdos(dee,see)        /* function declared */
int  dee;            /* variable to be passed to DE register */
     see;            /* variable to be passed to C register */

{
#asm
     POP H           /* get return address in HL */
     POP D           /* get DE parameter in DE */
     POP B           /* get C parameter in BC */

     PUSH B          /* resave stack to original state */
     PUSH D
     PUSH H

     CALL 0005H      /* call CP/M BDOS routine */
     MOV  L,A        /* insure that return status in A */
     MVI  H,0        /* clear H for return */

     RET             /* Not necessary or allowed by
                      * some compilers, which provide
                      * an automatic RET upon finding
                      * an ENDASM statement
                      */

#endasm
}                    */ end of BDOS function */
```

The issue of calling other labels from within assembly language imbedded in c source code requires you to know the format of the labels used by the compiler's assembler. Remember, the compiler is probably generating labels for its own internal (and external if you're also linking the code) use, and you don't want to duplicate a label unwittingly.

In general, it is best not to attempt to have your assembly language code refer to any labels generated by the c code compilation, since it requires you to know something about the internal architecture of the compiler (you may be violating register requirements).

Appendix C—Operating System Differences

At the time this book was written, c compilers are commonly available under three different operating environments:

- UNIX
- CP/M-80, CP/M-86, CP/M-68K
- MS-DOS

Compilers also exist for RSX-11, Flex, Apple DOS, and several other unique operating systems.

The following are the primary areas of difference between operating environments:

- c compiler invocation
- file naming conventions
- redirection facilities

c compiler invocation

In standard UNIX, the following is normally true:

/bin/as	filename of assembler
/bin/cc	filename of c compiler
/bin/lint	filename of c syntax checker
/bin/cb	filename of c program "beautifier"
/usr/src/libc/stdio	filename of standard I/O functions
/usr/src/libc/gen	filename of other general functions

The process of creating a c program under UNIX is the following:

1. Create source code file using ed.

2. Invoke the c compiler, which creates assembly language code, assembles this into object code, links the object code into executable code in a file named a.out.

3. If problems arise in the compilation or running of the program, use lint to run a syntax check.

See page 5 for a complete UNIX programming session. Under CP/M, the following is normally true:

cc.com	filename of c compiler	CP/M-80
cc.cmd		CP/M-86
asm.com	filename of assembler	CP/M-80
asm.cmd		CP/M-86
stdio.c	source code to standard I/O functions	
stdio.h		

The process of creating a c program under CP/M is the following:

1. Create source code using an editor (ED.COM).

2. Compile c code using CC.COM.

3. Assemble using ASM.COM (sometimes automatic).

4. Link using LINK.COM, CLINK.COM, or L80.COM (sometimes automatic).

See page 4 for a full programming session using CP/M versions of c. Under MS-DOS, the following is usually true:

```
cc.exe                    filename of c compiler
cc.com

masm.exe                  filename of assembler
masm.com
asm.ext
asm.com

stdio.c                   filename of I/O function source code
stdio.h
```

The following procedure is used to create a c program under MS-DOS:

1. Create the source code file using EDLIN.

2. Compile using CC.

3. Assemble using ASM (sometimes automatically called).

4. Link using LINK (sometimes automatically called).

The allowable options on the command line that invokes the c compiler vary with operating systems and compilers.

Appendix D—ASCII Character Chart

The ASCII (American Standard for Coded Information Interchange) codes are listed below in decimal, octal, hex, binary, and the ASCII definition.

DECIMAL	HEX	OCTAL	BINARY	DEFINITION	(MNEMONIC)
0	00	000	0000 0000	^@	NUL
1	01	001	0000 0001	^A	SOH
2	02	002	0000 0010	^B	STX
3	03	003	0000 0011	^C	ETX
4	04	004	0000 0100	^D	EOT
5	05	005	0000 0101	^E	ENQ
6	06	006	0000 0110	^F	ACK
7	07	007	0000 0111	^G	BEL
8	08	010	0000 1000	^H	BS
9	09	011	0000 1001	^I	HT
10	0A	012	0000 1010	^J	LF
11	0B	013	0000 1011	^K	VT
12	0C	014	0000 1100	^L	FF
13	0D	015	0000 1101	^M	CR
14	0E	016	0000 1110	^N	SO
15	0F	017	0000 1111	^O	SI
16	10	020	0001 0000	^P	DLE
17	11	021	0001 0001	^Q	DC1
18	12	022	0001 0010	^R	DC2
19	13	023	0001 0011	^S	DC3
20	14	024	0001 0100	^T	DC4
21	15	025	0001 0101	^U	NAK
22	16	026	0001 0110	^V	SYN
23	17	027	0001 0111	^W	ETB
24	18	030	0001 1000	^X	CAN
25	19	031	0001 1001	^Y	EM
26	1A	032	0001 1010	^Z	SUB
27	1B	033	0001 1011	ESCAPE	ESC
28	1C	034	0001 1100		FS
29	1D	035	0001 1101		GS
30	1E	036	0001 1110		RS
31	1F	037	0001 1111		US
32	20	040	0010 0000	SPACE	
33	21	041	0010 0001	!	
34	22	042	0010 0010	"	
35	23	043	0010 0011	#	
36	24	044	0010 0100	$	
37	25	045	0010 0101	%	
38	26	046	0010 0110	&	
39	27	047	0010 0111	'	
40	28	050	0010 1000	(	

DECIMAL	HEX	OCTAL	BINARY	DEFINITION (MNEMONIC)
41	29	051	0010 1001	)
42	2A	052	0010 1010	*
43	2B	053	0010 1011	+
44	2C	054	0010 1100	,
45	2D	055	0010 1101	-
46	2E	056	0010 1110	.
47	2F	057	0010 1111	/
48	30	060	0011 0000	0
49	31	061	0011 0001	1
50	32	062	0011 0010	2
51	33	063	0011 0011	3
52	34	064	0011 0100	4
53	35	065	0011 0101	5
54	36	066	0011 0110	6
55	37	067	0011 0111	7
56	38	070	0011 1000	8
57	39	071	0011 1001	9
58	3A	072	0011 1010	:
59	3B	073	0011 1011	;
60	3C	074	0011 1100	<
61	3D	075	0011 1101	=
62	3E	076	0011 1110	>
63	3F	077	0011 1111	?
64	40	100	0100 0000	@
65	41	101	0100 0001	A
66	42	102	0100 0010	B
67	43	103	0100 0011	C
68	44	104	0100 0100	D
69	45	105	0100 0101	E
70	46	106	0100 0110	F
71	47	107	0100 0111	G
72	48	110	0100 1000	H
73	49	111	0100 1001	I
74	4A	112	0100 1010	J
75	4B	113	0100 1011	K
76	4C	114	0100 1100	L
77	4D	115	0100 1101	M
78	4E	116	0100 1110	N
79	4F	117	0100 1111	O
80	50	120	0101 0000	P
81	51	121	0101 0001	Q
82	52	122	0101 0010	R
83	53	123	0101 0011	S
84	54	124	0101 0100	T
85	55	125	0101 0101	U

DECIMAL	HEX	OCTAL	BINARY	DEFINITION	(MNEMONIC)
86	56	126	0101 0110	V	
87	57	127	0101 0111	W	
88	58	130	0101 1000	X	
89	59	131	0101 1001	Y	
90	5A	132	0101 1010	Z	
91	5B	133	0101 1011	[	
92	5C	134	0101 1100	\	
93	5D	135	0101 1101	]	
94	5E	136	0101 1110	^	
95	5F	137	0101 1111	_	
96	60	140	0110 0000	'	
97	61	141	0110 0001	a	
98	62	142	0110 0010	b	
99	63	143	0110 0011	c	
100	64	144	0110 0100	d	
101	65	145	0110 0101	e	
102	66	146	0110 0110	f	
103	67	147	0110 0111	g	
104	68	150	0110 1000	h	
105	69	151	0110 1001	i	
106	6A	152	0110 1010	j	
107	6B	153	0110 1011	k	
108	6C	154	0110 1100	l	
109	6D	155	0110 1101	m	
110	6E	156	0110 1110	n	
111	6F	157	0110 1111	o	
112	70	160	0111 0000	p	
113	71	161	0111 0001	q	
114	72	162	0111 0010	r	
115	73	163	0111 0011	s	
116	74	164	0111 0100	t	
117	75	165	0111 0101	u	
118	76	166	0111 0110	v	
119	77	167	0111 0111	w	
120	78	170	0111 1000	x	
121	79	171	0111 1001	y	
122	7A	172	0111 1010	z	
123	7B	173	0111 1011	{	
124	7C	174	0111 1100			
125	7D	175	0111 1101	}	
126	7E	176	0111 1110	~	
127	7F	177	0111 1111	DELETE	DEL

Appendix E—printf and scanf Conversion Characters

The following is the order in which a printf conversion specification is presented:

```
First ------------------------------------------------------------------------------- > Last
PERCENT  MINUS  FIELD   PERIOD        NUMBER   LENGTH    CONVERSION
  SIGN         SIGN  WIDTH  SEPARATOR   CHARS    MODIFIER  CHARACTER
               DIGIT                   TO PRINT
Required <----------------------- Optional ----------------------> Required
```

A sample printf statement

```
printf("This is a conversion string: %-4.3d ",argument);
```

The order must be followed. You may omit any of the optional conversion specifications that appear between the percent sign and the conversion character, but the order must remain the same. NOTE: A period must appear before the "number of characters o print" field, or the printf function will interpret the number to be the field width specification.

The following are the definitions for the required and optional characters in the conversion string:

% The percent sign begins the conversion process. All characters up to the next space may be interpreted as being part of the conversion string. On most compilers, the first uninterpretable character ends the conversion string.

- The (optional) minus sign is used to specify that the converted argument should be left-justified in the specified field width.

n An (optional) number not preceded by a period is interpreted to be the field width; the width of the string in which the converted argument will be placed. The number should be in the integer range for the compiler in question. A zero preceding this number results in the printing of all leading zeroes for numeric arguments.

. The (optional) period is used to distinguish the field width specification from the next, also numeric, specification.

n A (optional) number following a period is interpreted to specify the number of characters to be printed (if the argument is a string), or the number of digits to the right of the decimal point (if the argument is a numeric data type like float or double). The number should be in the integer range for the compiler in question.

l A lowercase L, if present, is a length modifier and specifies that the argument in question is to be considered a long instead of integer.

x One of the following conversion characters:
    d   Argument is converted to decimal notation.

    o   Argument is converted to unsigned octal notation, with no leading zero.

x   Argument is converted to unsigned hexadecimal notation, with no leading 0x (in other words, C9, not 0xC9).

u   Argument is converted to unsigned decimal notation.

c   Argument is converted to a single character.

s   Argument is converted to a string.

e   Argument is converted to exponential notation, in the form -#.######E ± ##. Default precision to the right of the decimal point is 6 places on most compilers.

f   Argument is converted to floating point notation, in the form -###.######. Default precision to the right of the decimal point is 6 places on most compilers.

g   Argument is converted into either exponential or floating point format (see above), whichever results in the shorter string of characters. Non-significant zeroes are suppressed.

If a percent sign appears and the next character is not one of the appropriate ones described above, the next character is printed literally. A %% results in the printing of one percent sign in the resulting output string.

scanf conversion characters are similar to those of the printf function. The following is the order in which conversion characters should appear in a scanf input string:

first -- > last

PERCENT SIGN	NUMBER FOR FIELD LENGTH	LENGTH MODIFIER	CONVERSION CHARACTER
(required)	(optional)	(optional)	(required)

A sample scanf statement:

```
scanf("%5d %10s",arg1,arg2);
```

The allowable conversion characters are

d   decimal integer input
o   octal integer input (no leading zero)
x   hexadecimal integer input (no leading 0x)
h   a short integer input
c   a single character input
s   a character string input
f   a floating point input

In addition, assignment suppression is possible in the scanf function by placing a * (asterisk) immediately after the percent sign in the conversion string. When encountered, the next applicable input is ignored and not assigned to the next available argument (it is skipped over).

blank, tab, and newline characters are ignored in a scanf conversion string. Any other character in the conversion string that is not part of a conversion specification specifies the next character input must match that character exactly, or an error should be reported.

Appendix F—Common c Definition File (standard.h)

```
/* The following is the source code to a number of common
 *definitions used by c programmers. Some of these may already
 * be defined by your compiler, others may not be present. It
 * is recommended practice that each organization or individual
 * who uses c create their own common definition file and #include
 * it in each program they create.
 */

/* numeric constants */
#define FALSE      0                    /* logical false */
#define TRUE       !FALSE               /* logical true */
#define NULL       0                    /* when used for numeric value */
#define EOF        -1                   /* end of file marker */
#define YES        1                    /* alternative name: TRUE */
#define NO         0                    /* alternative name: FALSE */
#define SUCCEED    0
#define FAIL       1                    /* alternative value: -1 */
#define PAGELEN    66                   /* standard page length */
#define CRTWIDTH   80                   /* standard CRT width */
#define MAXFILE    3                    /* maximum number of files open */


/* program macro functions */
#define MAX(a,b)   ((a)<(b) ? (b) : (a))
#define MIN(a,b)   ((a)<(b) ? (a) : (b))
#define ABS(a)     ((a)>0 ? (a) : -(a))
#define EQUALS     = =
#define AND        &&
#define OR         ||
#define NOTHING;   ;                    /* used for null statements */
#define GETCHAR()  getc(stdin)
#define PUTCHAR(x) putc(x,stdout)
#define FOREVER    for(;;)              /* endless loop */
#define BEGIN      {                    /*for Pascal programmers */
#define END        }                    /* for Pascal programmers */
#define GETLN(s,n) ((fgets(s,n,stdin)) = =NULL ? EOF : strlen(s))

/* user-created (derived) data types */
#define ushort     unsigned short
#define bits       ushort
#define bool       int
#define metachar   short
#define void       int

/* some alternative user-created (derived) data type definitions
 *
 * typedef short ushort;
 * typedef char       tiny;
 * typedef char       utiny;
 * typedef int        void;
 * #define ushort(n)  ((unsigned)((n) & 0xFFFF))
 * #define tiny(n)    (((n) & 0x80) ? (~0x7F (n)) | : (n))
 * #define utiny(n)   ((n) & 0xFF)
 */
```

Appendix G—Definitions for User-Created Data Types

bits

Name

bits

Format

```
bits name;
bits name-list;
class bits name;
class bits name-list;
```

Purpose

The bits data type is a derived type to be used solely for bitwise operation.

Usage Rules

1. A bits data type is usually the same as if the variable had been declared as an unsigned short (16 bits, with no sign bit used).

2. Programmers feel it is important to use the bits data type to remind themselves that the value stored in the variable is used only for bitwise operations and manipulations, and does not contain any other valid information.

Defaults

None.

Example

Sample use:

```
typedef unsigned short bits;
bits drill;
drill <<= 0x01;
```

Exceptions

Compilers do not have a bits definition; the programmer must create it.

Returns

Not applicable.

bool

Name

bool

Format

```
bool name;
bool name-list;
class bool name;
class bool name-list;
```

Purpose

The bool data type is a derived type used only for the storage of Boolean values (TRUE or FALSE, nominally non-zero and zero).

Usage Rules

1. A bool type variable is generally the same as if it had been defined as a short int.

2. Programmers feel it is important to use this derived type to remind themselves that the value stored in a bool type variable is used for storing only TRUE or FALSE values. No other values should be placed in a bool type variable.

Defaults

None.

Example

Sample use:

```
typedef short int bool;
bool leon;
leon = getchar(c) <= 45;
```

Exceptions

Compilers do not have a bool data type. The programmer must create it. Some programmers allow only ones (TRUE) and zeroes (FALSE) to be stored in a bool type variable, while others use the definitions of non-zero (TRUE) and zero (FALSE).

Returns

Not applicable.

bits

bool

metachar

Name

metachar

Format

```
metachar name;
metachar name-list;
class metachar name;
class metachar name-list;
```

Purpose

The metachar data type is a derived type used to receive returned values from a function that may be an ASCII character or an EOF (-1) value.

Usage Rules

1. The metachar data type is the same as a signed int variable.

2. Programmers use metachar data types to remind themselves that a function may return something other than an ASCII character.

Defaults

None.

Example

Sample use:

```
typedef int metachar;
metachar &atable;
```

Exceptions

Compilers do not include a metachar data type. It must be created by the programmer.

Returns

Not applicable.

tbool

Name

tbool

Format

```
tbool name;
tbool name-list;
class tbool name;
class tbool name-list;
```

Purpose

The tbool derived data type uses less storage space than bool to store the same Boolean values (TRUE or FALSE, non-zero or zero).

Usage Rules

1. The tbool (stands for tiny Boolean) data type is generally the same as a char (a one-byte character), but is used only to store a Boolean value.

2. Programmers use tbool data types to remind themselves that the only valid data values stored by the variable are Boolean values (non-zero for TRUE and zero for FALSE). tbool is used instead of type bool when memory space is at a premium.

Defaults

None.

Example

Sample use:

```
typedef char tbool;
tbool = (fedres < prime);
```

Exceptions

Compilers do not include a tbool data type. It must be created by the programmer.

Returns

Not applicable.

metachar

tbool

ushort

Name

ushort

Format

```
ushort name;
ushort name-list;
class ushort name;
class ushort name-list;
```

Purpose

The ushort data type is a derived data type used to store short, unsigned integers.

Usage Rules

1. The ushort data type is the same as a data type of unsigned short. Normally, this means ushort variables contain 16 bits of information, with no bits used to store the sign of the value.

2. Programmers use the ushort derived type to remind themselves that an unsigned integer value is stored by the variable.

Defaults

None.

Example

Sample use:

```
typedef unsigned short ushort;
static int metall = 6;
ushort = metall - 1;
```

Exceptions

Compilers do not include a tbool data type. It must be created by the programmer.

Returns

Not applicable.

void

Name

void

Format

```
void function-name(arguments)
```

Purpose

The void derived data type is used to declare that the function it relates to does not return a value of any kind.

Usage Rules

1. void is normally the same as the signed int data type, the default for most c compilers.

2. Programmers use void data types in defining functions to clearly remind themselves that no value is expected to be returned from the function.

Defaults

None.

Example

Sample use:

```
typedef int void;
void cursor(x,y)
int x,y;
{
    putchar(0x1b);
    putchar('=');
    putchar(x);
    putchar(y);
}
```

Exceptions

Current release UNIX c compilers implement void as a keyword for use in declaring functions that do not return anything. On these newer UNIX compilers, void is *not* the same as unsigned int, being instead a null data type.

Returns

Not applicable.

ushort

void

Appendix H—Example Function Libraries (string.h)

```
/*  string.h
 *
 *  This file contains the following common string functions:
 *
 *          strlen
 *          strcat
 *          strcpy
 *          strcmp
 *          indexc
 *
 *  Please note these functions do not have extensive
 *  error checking in them. Alternates for some of these
 *  functions may be found in Kernighan and Ritchie's book,
 *  and Thomas Plum's book.
 *
 *  This file requires that standard.h (see Appendix F)
 *  be included into the program.
 *
 */


/* --------------------------------------------------------------
 *  unsigned strlen(string)
 *
 *  The strlen function returns the length of the string
 *  referred to in the argument list.
 *
 */
unsigned strlen(s)
char *s;
{
        int count;

        for(count = 0; *s++ count++)
                ;
        return count;
}



/* --------------------------------------------------------------
 *  void strcat(string1,string2)
 *
 *  The strcat function concatenates (adds) the second
 *  string to the end of the first string. NOTE: The
 *  first string must have been declared with enough
 *  room to hold both strings!
 *
 */
void strcat(s,t)
char *s, *t;
{
    for(;*s; s++)              /* get to end of first string */
        ;
    do
    {
        *s++ = *t;            /* copy character, then increment s */
    }
    while (*t++);             /* check if done, else increment */
}
```

```
/* ------------------------------------------------------------
 * void strcpy(string1,string2)
 *
 * The strcpy function copies the second string into the
 * first string's allocated space (the first string
 * becomes the second).
 */
void strcpy(s,t)
char *s, *t;
{
        do
        {
        *  s++=*t;         /* copy the character, then increment s */

        }
        while(*t++);        /* check if at end of t, else increment t */

}
/* ------------------------------------------------------------
 * int strcmp(string1,string2)
 *
 * The strcmp function compares the characters in two strings.
 * A zero is returned if the strings are identical. A value
 * of less than zero is returned if the first different
 * character in string1 is lower in ASCII value than its
 * corresponding character in string2. A value of greater than zero
 * is returned if the first different character in string1
 * is higher in ASCII value than its corresponding character
 * in string2.
 *
 */
    int strcmp(s,t)
    char *s, *t;
    {
        for ( ;*s == *t; s++, t++)
            if (*s == '\0')
                    return 0;
        return (*s - *t);
    }


/* ------------------------------------------------------------
 * int indexc(string1,character)
 *
 * The indexc function returns the position in string1 of the
 * location of the character, or, if the character is not
 * contained within string1, a -1 is returned. Note: This
 * test is machine word size dependent.
 *
 */
    int indexc(s,c)
    char s[], c;
    {
        int point;
        for(point = 0; s[point]; point++)
        {
            if(s[point] == c)
                return point;
        }
        return -1
    }
```

```
/*  is.h
 *
 *  This file contains the following functions:
 *          islower
 *          isupper
 *          isalpha
 *          isdigit
 *          isalnum
 *          isspace
 *          ispunct
 *          isprint
 *          iscntrl
 *          isascii
 *          toupper
 *          tolower
 *
 *  These functions do not do any error checking and
 *  certainly aren't very sophisticated. They are here
 *  to show you what a simple is function library might
 *  look like.
 *
 *  This file requires that standard.h (see Appendix F)
 *  be "included" into the program.
 */


/* ----------------------------------------------------------------
 *  bool isdigit(character)
 *
 *  This function determines whether or not the character
 *  in question is a digit (0 to 9, inclusive). Returns TRUE if the
 *  character is a digit, 0 otherwise.
 *
 */
bool isdigit(c)
char c;
{
    return (('0' <= c && c <= '9')? TRUE : FALSE);
}


/* ----------------------------------------------------------------
 *  bool isupper(character)
 *
 *  The isupper function determines whether or not the
 *  character in question is an uppercase letter. Returns
 *  1 if the character is uppercase, 0 otherwise.
 *
 */
bool isupper(c)
char c;
{
    return (('A' <= c && c <= 'Z')? TRUE : FALSE);
}
/* ----------------------------------------------------------------
 *  bool islower(character)
 *
 *  The islower function determines whether or not the
 *  character in question is a lowercase letter. Returns
 *  1 if the character is lowercase, 0 otherwise.
 *
 */
bool islower(c)
char c;
{
```

```
    return (('a' <= c && c <= 'z') ? TRUE : FALSE);
}


/* ----------------------------------------------------------------
 *  bool isalpha(character)
 *
 *  The isalpha function determines whether or not the
 *  character in question is a letter. Returns TRUE
 *  if the character is a letter, 0 otherwise.
 *
 */
bool isalpha(c)
char c;
{
    return ((('A' <= c && c <= 'Z') ||
            ('a' <= c && c <= 'z'))? TRUE : FALSE) ;
}



/* ----------------------------------------------------------------
 *  bool isalnum(character)
 *
 *  The isalnum function determines whether or not the
 *  character in question is a number or letter. Returns
 *  1 if the character is a number or letter, 0 otherwise.
 *
 */
bool isalnum(c)
char c;
{
    return ((('a' <= c && c <= 'z') ||
            ('A' <= c && c <= 'Z') ||
            ('0' <= c && c <= '9'))? TRUE : FALSE);
}



/* ----------------------------------------------------------------
 *  bool isspace(character)
 *
 *  The isspace function determines whether or not the
 *  character in question is a space, tab, carriage return,
 *  form feed, or newline character. Returns TRUE if the
 *  character is one of these, 0 otherwise.
 *
 */
bool isspace(c)
char c;
{
    return (((c == ' ') ||
            (c == '\n') ||
            (c == '\t') ||
            (c == '\f') ||
            (c == '\r'))? TRUE : FALSE);
}



/* ----------------------------------------------------------------
 *  bool ispunct(character)
 *
 *  The ispunct function determines whether or not the
 *  character in question is a punctuation character
```

```
 *  ( . , : ; ! ? and so on). Returns TRUE if it is, 0 otherwise.
 *
 */
bool ispunct(c)
char c;
{
    return (((('!' <= c && c <= '/')  ||
              (':' <= c && c <= '@')  ||
              ('[' <= c && c <= '`')  ||
              ('{' <= c && c <= '~'))? TRUE : FALSE) ;
}



/* ----------------------------------------------------------------
 *  bool iscntrl(character)
 *
 *  The iscntrl function determines whether or not the
 *  character in question is a legal control character
 *  (ASCII 0 through 31) or the DEL key (ASCII 127), Returns TRUE if
 *  it is, 0 otherwise.
 *
 */
bool iscntrl(c)
char c;
{
    return ((( 127 == c) ||
            (0 <= c && c <= 31))? TRUE : FALSE) ;

}



/* ----------------------------------------------------------------
 *  bool isascii(character)
 *
 *  The isascii function determines whether or not the
 *  character in question is a character in the ASCII
 *  character set (ASCII 0 through 127). Returns TRUE
 *  if it is, 0 otherwise.
 *
 */
bool isascii(c)
char c;
{
    return (( 0 <= c && c < 128)? TRUE : FALSE);
}

/* ----------------------------------------------------------------
 * bool isprint(character)
 *
 *  the isprint function determines whether or not the
 *  character in question is a printable ASCII character
 *  (ASCII 32 through 126, all other values are control
 *  or function characters. Returns TRUE if it is, 0
 *  otherwise.
 *
 */
bool isprint(c)
char c;
}
    return (('  ' <= c && c <= '~')? TRUE : FALSE);
}
```

```
/* ----------------------------------------------------------
 *
 *  char toupper(c)
 *  Returns uppercase equivalent of character, or, if the
 *  original character is not lowercase, the character is returned
 *  unchanged.
 *
 */
char toupper(c)
char c;
{
    return islower(c) ? c-32 : c;
}




/* ----------------------------------------------------------
 *
 *  char tolower(c)
 *
 *  Returns lowercase equivalent of character, or, if the
 *  original character is not uppercase, the character is returned
 *  unchanged.
 */
char tolower(c)
char c;
{
    return isupper(c) ? c+32 : c;
}
```

Index